Contents

Chapter 1

Visualization and Digital Collections

Since the 1990s, cultural heritage institutions have been investing in digital technologies to address a growing public demand for open and permanent access to information resources. Accordingly, galleries, libraries, archives, and museums worldwide have strategically focused on the digitization of their holdings. The next step involved the development of digital collections and services in support of online research and learning.[1]

While enabling direct access to cultural and scientific heritage, digitization of archival materials has also fostered their preservation, virtual collocation on web portals, and the creation of an integrated learning environment. As a result, libraries have seen a substantial increase in the use of digitized materials that have attracted diverse users.[2] Researchers, scholars, educators, entrepreneurs, and web surfers have engaged with content on an unprecedented scale because it is available in digital format.[3]

This digital shift in the library world continues to accelerate. Due to the pandemic crisis in 2020, print collections have rapidly become unavailable. Research and learning have moved to a virtual environment for the immediate future, and perhaps for good. Digital content has suddenly transitioned from being a preview of the physical collection to its primary access point.[4]

Digital collections, however, are not simply representations of physical collections. Rather, they are resources in their own right.[5] Unlike physical collections, digital ones have detailed metadata and, often, full text available due to OCR conversion of text images into machine-encoded data. Both metadata and data can be mined, analyzed, and visualized. *Text mining* refers to discovering and extracting meaningful patterns from large numbers of text documents. Practitioners of computational linguistics and digital humanities call these agglomerations of texts *corpora* or *capta*.[6] Text analysis of *corpora* or *capta* at its very basic level involves looking at words' frequencies, contexts, lexical preferences, and relations among textual elements. *Visualization* refers to the design of the graphic representations of data objects and their relationships.[7] It is commonly viewed as an essential part of textual data analysis that helps to make quantitative information legible and easy to comprehend.[8]

Digital collections' data are open for exploration and analysis just as any other data are. Similarly to humanists, who now examine how technology is changing our understanding of the liberal arts, we can employ digital tools to see how they may shape our understanding of archival curation and librarianship.[9] We begin with examining some pragmatic reasons for visualization of digital collections. Then our focus will move to the particular application of visualization tools, specifically the R programming language, including ggpolt2 and RShiny. R has been designed to facilitate data analysis, statistics, statistical programming, and graphics.[10]

Why Visualize a Digital Collection's Data

There are multiple reasons to visualize a digital collection's data, but one of the most important is to appeal to our natural visual abilities. Humans are very good at seeing patterns. The biggest part of our brain cortex is involved in visual perception.[11] According to the Light Switch Theory by Andrew Parker, the eyes and vision have been the primal driving force of biological evolution since the Cambrian Period, approximately 543 million years ago.[12] The rapid development of visual perception has thus been considered a fundamental survival strategy for animal species, including humans. Tuned by evolution, human vision has always been our most critical sense for detecting and extracting information from our physical surroundings.[13]

Naturally, various forms of visualization, as means of communication utilized by people, have been present worldwide throughout human history. Cave paintings and rock art, maps, calendars, genealogical trees, chronological tables, and time lines, as well as modern-day charts and graphs, have all been used to convey essential information so that it can be grasped quickly.[14] This high efficiency of an image that "is worth a thousand words" has recently played a leading role in the development of present-day screen culture. In his book on this global phenomenon, Richard Butsch formally defines *screen culture* and points to its continuing relevance:

> Screens are about images more than language, a modern form of visual culture. . . . It is the *lived* culture that arises when people interact with and through screen media. As everyday life fills with screen activity—averaging nine hours per day for American adults in 2017—screen becomes an increasingly important aspect of the broader culture infiltrating and influencing all other elements.[15]

Indeed, visualization presently seems to dominate all communications.[16] Films, television, video games, video websites, mobile applications, and social media circulate images on a massive scale. We interact with dashboards, maps, newspaper charts, app graphs, and text messages enhanced by emojis or animated GIFs on an hourly basis. Visual representations have become an integral part of our social and professional communication practices. Scott Berinato refers to visualization as a lingua franca used in knowledge economies of the twenty-first century.[17] He argues that the attractiveness of visualization stems from its ability to summarize and simplify complex data and thus help to make sense of them. In addition, the practice of data visualization has now been demystified and democratized.[18] It is no longer in the purview of only software experts and professional coders. Due to technological advances and growing demand, tools for creating graphs and charts have become open and available to everyone who is willing to learn a new language.[19] If libraries are to participate and contribute to screen culture, then perhaps it is time to learn its language and go visual.

There is a growing literature on the relevance of graphics for digital libraries. Visualization is often used to support exploration and discovery, content analysis, and communication about the collection. For example, graphical representations of digital collections are considered to be a great alternative to text-based interfaces and search boxes, especially for non-experts and casual users.[20] Unlike empty search fields that rely on the users' input and background knowledge, graphs and diagrams provide a comprehensive overview of the collection easily understandable by all users. Along the same lines, "generous interfaces" are designed to show graphs of digital collections up front on web portals in order to both spark users' interest and inspire further exploration of digitized material.[21] In addition to providing an overview of a collection's scope and content, generous interfaces include the contexts for the collection, a display of the relationships among collection items, and a quick closer look at selected images. These graphic overviews are natural starting points for browsing large sets of digital items, identifying relevant topics and patterns, selecting pertinent documents and images, and finally focusing on their details.[22] Recent implementations of visual search and discovery involve interactive interfaces where users navigate digital collections as virtual galleries.[23] According to Eric Phettelace, interactivity adds an additional discovery layer that enables users to become active agents in finding new patterns in data and putting new interpretations on them.[24]

Indeed, graphics foster not only intended searches for information, but also serendipitous findings. According to Windhager and colleagues, following graphics and diagrams often leads users to discoveries of diverse perspectives about a collection's data.[25] These unexpected findings, in turn, may inspire new approaches to examination of historical evidence and new ways of thinking about the nature of primary sources and information at large. Since charts and diagrams may easily reflect a diversity of views and the complexity of information, they seem to be very well suited for multithreaded investigation.[26]

Similarly, archivists and curators find the application of graphics extremely useful for the analysis of large digital collections.[27] Visualization allows curators to examine the structure and organization of a collection, its content and provenance, relationships among the collection's items, the scope and size of the collection, and the number of files and their formats, as well as text patterns in documents and visual patterns among images. In addition, graphs may reveal distributions of various documents and images over time that provide remarkable insight into the process of collection development. Monitoring progress of a collection also involves the assessment of its metadata in terms of their completeness and quality. Computing applications used for visualization fully expose all inconsistencies and missing values across metadata fields. Visualization then may also be used as an effective tool for metadata quality control. All these observations about a collection's structure and a description of its content come with a growing understanding of data enabled by visualization. Richard Hamming once pointed out that the purpose of computing is insight—not numbers.[28] By the same token, the purpose of visualization is grasp rather than graphics.

To enable readers to get a good grasp on data, graphics need to communicate information clearly. Graphs and diagrams are to explain data, not to obscure them.[29] According to Richie Cotton, the effectiveness of a plot can be measured by two criteria: how many insights readers can get from the plot and how fast they can do so.[30] Some plots are specifically designed to tell stories. There seems to be a strong relationship between data, visualization, and narrative, especially when it comes to graphic representation of time and chronology.[31] The concept of mapping duration to space, and particularly to the length of a line, was first put into practice by Joseph Priestly in 1764 to compare the life spans of 2,000 famous people.[32] The idea of time represented by a measurable line has evolved ever since, reflected in drawn streams, chains, trees, and now time lines. Time has become an organizing principle for diagrams. But it is also the organizing principle for narratives. Like graphs, narratives represent events in time.[33] Like graphs, stories help people see.

Digital data have their own stories to tell.[34] They also have their own ways of doing so. Traditionally, graphs and diagrams have been used to support narratives with envisioned concrete evidence embedded in a text sequence. This sequence usually starts with an overview of data in order to set the scene and context for their interpretation. After setting the opening scene, the creator of a graph guides the readers through its most prominent features and smoothly directs users' attention from one point of interest to the next one. Less prominent data features, which do not add to the main story, are typically left out, as the author tries to present the data in the most convincing way to advance the line of a given argument. However, the full complexity of digital data may not be adequately represented by one leading story line.[35] Rather, it calls for multiple interpretations depending on readers' interests. Once again interactivity of graphs seems to invite and enable users to create their own story lines and paths of discovery. The plots developed by users may diverge considerably from the order suggested by authors and follow various unexpected directions. Users may remix data and reinvent the entire interpretation of a collection. A combination of a traditional narrative approach and interactive elements that foster user-driven exploration is becoming a standard in designing visual representations.

Indeed, visual communication tends to work best when the audience gets engaged in the communication process.[36] Clearly, active learning radically improves comprehension of data. It also awakens users' curiosity. The key objective for developing visualizations of digital collections should then be to inspire and actively engage users with digital content. But the users need to be familiar with visual interfaces and feel comfortable interacting with them in the first place.[37]

The GLAM Labs community provides support for users seeking to feel more comfortable interacting with visualizations.[38] Galleries, libraries, archives, and museums (GLAM) have promoted digital content for reuse and experimentation in educational, commercial, and artistic projects. For the GLAM Labs community, digital cultural heritage is not just to contemplate, but also to fully engage with in creative ways. Accordingly, Europeana Pro, the British Library Digital Scholarship Department, the Library of Congress's LC Labs, and the Digital Public Library of America—DPLA Pro all now offer comprehensive guidelines for how to work and innovate with digital collections.[39]

The development of digital cultural heritage agglomerations, like the Europeana Project that started in 2007 and the DPLA established in 2010, have paralleled the rise of the digital humanities (DH) as a new research field with its own questions and methodology. Digital collections are primary research sources for DH scholars, whereas data visualization is one of their essential methods for text and data analysis.[40] Anne Burdick and her associates argue that visualization in fact provides "graphical legibility to analytical results."[41] In their view, geo-temporal visualizations and mapping allow scholars to examine complex interrelations among cultural, social, and historical phenomena.

In contrast with a traditional humanities research approach that emphasizes individual authorship, a digital approach fosters cooperation and partnership. Based on a survey of five hundred scholars, librarians, and archivists, Jessica Wagner Webster shows that there are multiple opportunities for successful collaboration among these stakeholders in regard to digital projects.[42] Interestingly, the roles that these stakeholders play do not always align with expected tasks, in which DH scholars come up with research questions and interpret the results, while librarians and archivists are in charge of digital tools and their implementation. One of the benefits of interdisciplinary projects is a variety of views brought together. This is exactly where innovation begins.

A Process for Getting to Know Data

As discussed earlier, graphic representation is among our most important tools for organizing data and sharing information. The process of creating effective visualizations of given data involves some important preliminary steps, including selecting visualization tools and preprocessing data compiled in a table. The first step of this preprocessing is examining the data table and getting familiar with collection data and metadata. Gaining detailed knowledge about data allows consideration of which aspects of information contained in the data might be of interest to collection users or curators.

One of the tools that may help a user to get a clear insight about collection data is OpenRefine.[43] It is a free, open source software application for working with raw and messy data. OpenRefine allows for importing data in various formats, exploring large data sets, cleaning and transforming data, and also linking data sets with web services: for instance, getting geographic coordinates for addresses. OpenRefine runs on all major operating systems, including Windows, macOs, and Linux.

An OpenRefine project operates similarly to a spreadsheet or a table consisting of columns with metadata elements and rows of data. The rows can be filtered by various criteria and can also be edited. OpenRefine allows for detailed examination of the collection content and its description.

After examining data, the next step involves developing specific questions about a digital collection that compiled data may potentially address. In fact, these questions inform the initial mining of raw data and metadata. For this reason, this is the stage where interdisciplinary collaboration is particularly relevant because it brings diverse interests and questions together. Depending on the questions asked, the relevant pieces of information are extracted from the data table. These selected pieces are then closely examined for completeness and consistency. By nature all data, including metadata, tend to be messy. Therefore cleaning or tidying data is an essential prerequisite for their effective visual display.

Following data cleanup, the next step, often necessary, is transforming data. Data transformation allows for obtaining defined values necessary for plotting and graphic display. For example, extracting time measures in specific units from string date representations, aggregating data points according to different categories, and applying mathematical formulas to column values may be needed to obtain well-defined sets of specific numbers. The graphs are created by subjecting clean and transformed data to plotting functions that translate numbers into their graphic representations. The final step in the visualization process is tuning graphs for clarity.

As mentioned earlier, the number of tools for visualization is continually increasing. Many of them, including IBM Many Eyes, Library of Congress Viewshare, Microsoft Excel, Tableau, D3.js, FusionCharts, Google Charts, Dygraphs, Infogram, Plotly, IBM Watson Analytics, Tableau Public, TimelineJS, StorymapJS, Google Maps, and Historypin are discussed elsewhere.[44]

This report focuses on the application of the R programming language and its specific packages—ggplot2 for visualization and RShiny for interactive visualization. The next chapter addresses the methodology of learning the R programming language, the general workflow for basic visualization, and an introduction to graphic representations of data that serve specific analytical tasks.

Acknowledgments

I would like to thank Robert Weyrauch for inspiration to learn and use R, Pawel Musial for his guidance and patience, Ellen Bosman for her active support for this project, and also Matthew Martinez and Tiffany Schirmer, along with all current and former team members at NMSU Library, for their tremendous work on the Tombaugh Papers Collection.

Notes

1. Daniel Greenstein, "Digital Libraries and Their Challenges," *Library Trends* 49, no. 4 (2000): 290–303; Laura Deal, "Visualizing Digital Collections," *Technical Services Quarterly* 32 (2015):14–34; "IFLA/UNESCO Manifesto for Digital Libraries," International Federation of Library Associations and Institutions, accessed May 20, 2020, https://www.ifla.org/publications/iflaunesco-manifesto-for-digital-libraries; Florian Windhager, Paolo Federico, Günther Schreder, Katrin Glinka, Marian Dörk, Silvia Miksch, and Eva Mayr, "Visualization of Cultural Heritage Collection Data: State of the Art and Future Challenges," *IEEE Transactions on Visualization and Computer Graphics* 25, no. 6 (2019): 2311–2330, https://doi.org/10.1109/TVCG.2018.2830759.
2. Peter B. Hirtle, "The Impact of Digitization on Special Collections in Libraries," *Libraries & Culture: A Journal of Library History* 37, no. 1 (2002): 42–52, https://hdl.handle.net/1813/14206.
3. M. Mahey, A. Al-Abdulla, S. Ames, P. Bray, G. Candela, S. Chambers, C. Derven, et al., *Open a GLAM Lab* (Doha, Qatar: Qatar University Press, 2019), https://glamlabs.pubpub.org/.
4. Christopher Cox, "Changed, Changed Utterly," *Inside Higher Ed,* #Views, #Opinion, June 5, 2020, https://www.insidehighered.com/views/2020/06/05/academic-libraries-will-change-significant-ways-result-pandemic-opinion.
5. Florian Kräutli, "Visualising Cultural Data: Exploring Digital Collections through Timeline Visualisations" (doctoral thesis, Royal College of Art, London, 2016), http://www.kraeutli.com/index.php/2016/04/15/visualising-cultural-data/.
6. David Crystal, *The Cambridge Encyclopedia of Language*, 3rd ed. (New York: Cambridge University Press: 2010), 434–435;Johanna Drucker, "Digital Humanities: Approaches to Graphical Display," *DHQ: Digital Humanities Quarterly* 5, no. 11 (2011), http://www.digitalhumanities.org//dhq/vol/5/1/000091/000091.html; Anne Burdick, Johanna Drucker, Peter Lunenfeld, Todd Presner, and Jeffrey Schnapp, *Digital Humanities* (Cambridge, MA: MIT Press, 2012).
7. Katy Börner, Chaomei Chen, and Kevin W. Boyack, "Visualizing Knowledge Domains," *Annual Review of Information Science and Technology* 37, no. 1 (2003):

179–255, https://doi.org/10.1002/aris.1440370106.
8. Johanna Drucker, "5B. Data Mining and Text Analysis," in Johanna Drucker with David Kim, Iman Salehian, and Anthony Bushong, *Introduction to Digital Humanities: Concepts, Methods, and Tutorials for Students and Instructors*, course book for DH 101: Intro to Digital Humanities (Los Angeles, CA: UCLA Center for Digital Humanities, 2014), 43–45, http://dh101.humanities.ucla.edu/?page_id=48; Scott Berinato, *Good Charts: The HRB Guide to Making Smarter, More Persuasive Data Visualizations*, (Boston: Harvard Business Review Press, 2016).
9. Patricia Cohen, "Humanities 2.0: Digital Keys for Unlocking the Humanities' Riches," *New York Times*, November 16, 2010, https://www.nytimes.com/2010/11/17/arts/17digital.html?auth=link-dismiss-google1tap.
10. Hadley Wickham and Garrett Grolemund, *R for Data Science: Import, Tidy, Transform, Visualize and Model Data* (Sebastopol, CA: O'Reilly Media, 2017); J. D. Long and Paul Teetor, *R Cookbook: Proven Recipes for Data Analysis, Statistics and Graphics* (Sebastopol, CA: O'Reilly Media, Inc., 2019).
11. Margaret S. Livingstone, *Vision and Art: The Biology of Seeing*, rev. and exp. ed. (New York: Abrams, 2014).
12. Andrew Parker, *In the Blink of an Eye: How Vision Sparked the Big Bang of Evolution* (Cambridge, MA: Perseus, 2003).
13. Livingstone, *Vision and Art*; William S. Cleveland and Robert McGill, "Graphical Perception: Theory Experimentation and Application to the Development of Graphical Methods," *Journal of the American Statistical Association* 79, no. 387 (1984): 531–54; William S. Cleveland and Robert McGill, "Graphical Perception and Graphical Methods for Analyzing Scientific Data," *Science* 229 (August 30, 1985): 828–33.
14. Michael Friendly, "Milestone in the History of Data Visualization: A Case Study," in *Classification: The Ubiquitous Challenge: Proceedings of the 28th Annual Conference of the Gesellschaft für Klassifikation e.V., University of Dortmund, March 9–11, 2004*, ed. Claus Weihs and Wolfgang Gaul, 34–52 (Heidelberg, Germany: Springer-Verlag, 2005); Daniel Rosenberg and Anthony Grafton, *Cartographies of Time: A History of the Timeline* (New York: Princeton Architectural Press, 2010); Stephen Boyd Davis, Olivia Vane, and Florian Kräutli, "Using Data Visualisation to Tell Stories about Collections" (paper, Electronic Visualisation and the Arts [EVA] conference, London, UK, July 12–14, 2016), https://doi.org/10.14236/ewic/EVA2016.44; Berinato, *Good Charts*; Hsuanwei Michelle Chen, "Information Visualization," *Library Technology Reports* 53, no. 3 (April 2017).
15. Richard Butsch, *Screen Culture: A Global History* (Cambridge, UK Polity Press, 2019): 2–3.
16. Berinato, *Good Charts*.
17. Berinato, *Good Charts*.
18. Eric Phettelace, "Effectively Visualizing Library Data," *Reference and User Services Quarterly* 52, no. 2 (2012): 93–97.
19. Jannette L. Finch and Angela R. Flenner, "Using Data Visualization to Examine an Academic Library Collection," *College and Research Libraries* 77, no. 6 (2016): 765, https://doi.org/10.5860/crl.77.6.765; Chen, "Information Visualization;" Kayla Harris and Andrew Harris, "Data Visualization Tools for Archives and Special Collections," *MAC Newsletter*, Midwest Archives Conference, 2019: 26–29, https://ecommons.udayton.edu/imri_faculty_publications/39.
20. Panayiotis Zaphiris, Kulvinder Gill, Terry H. Y Ma, Stephanie Wilson, and Helen Petrie, "Exploring the Use of Information Visualization for Digital Libraries," *New Review of Information Networking* 10, no. 1 (2004): 51–69, https://doi.org/10.1080/1361457042000304136; Ali Shiri, "Metadata-Enhanced Visual Interfaces to Digital Libraries," *Journal of Information Science* 34, no. 6 (2008): 763–75, https://doi.org/10.1177/0165551507087711; Mitchell Whitelaw, "Towards Generous Interfaces for Archival Collections," (paper presented at the International Council on Archives Congress, Brisbane, Australia, August 20–24, 2012), http://mtchl.net/assets/Whitelaw_ICA_GenerousInterfaces.pdf; Deal, "Visualizing Digital Collections"; Florian Windhager, Paolo Federico, Eva Mayr, Günther Schreder and Michael Smuc, "A Review of Information Visualization Approaches and Interfaces to Digital Cultural Heritage Collections," in *Proceedings of the 9th Forum Media Technology 2016 and 2nd All Around Audio Symposium (FMT 2016), St. Pölten, Austria, November 23–24, 2016*, ed. Wolfgang Aigner, Grischa Schmiedl, Kerstin Blumenstein, Matthias Zeppelzauer, and Michael Iber, *CEUR Workshop Proceedings*, http://ceur-ws.org/Vol-1734/fmt-proceedings-2016-paper9.pdf; Windhager et al., "Visualization of Cultural Heritage Collection Data."
21. Whitelaw, "Towards Generous Interfaces."
22. Zaphiris et al., "Exploring the Use of Information"; Mark Hall and Paul Clough, "Exploring Large Digital Library Collections Using a Map-Based Visualisation," in *Research and Advanced Technology for Digital Libraries: International Conference on Theory and Practice of Digital Libraries, TPDL 2013, Valetta, Malta, September 22–26, 2013, Proceedings*, ed. Trond Aalberg, Christos Papatheodorou, Milena Dobreva, Giannis Tsakonas, and Charles J. Farrugia, 216–27, *Lecture Notes in Computer Science* 8092, (Berlin, Heidelberg: Springer, 2013); Deal, "Visualizing Digital Collections"; I. di Lenardo, B. Seguin, and F. Kaplan, "Visual Patterns Discovery in Large Databases of Paintings." Digital Humanities 2016: Conference Abstracts (Kraków: Jagiellonian University and Pedagogical University, 2016): 169–72, https://dh2016.adho.org/abstracts/348.
23. Jeffrey P. Emanuel, Christopher M. Morse, and Luke Hollis, "The New Interactive: Reimagining Visual Collections as Immersive Environments," *VRA Bulletin* 43, no. 2, (2016), article 2, https://online.vraweb.org/index.php/vrab/article/view/52/57.
24. Phettelace, "Effectively Visualizing Library Data."
25. Windhager et al., "Visualization of Cultural Heritage Collection Data."
26. Shiri, "Metadata-Enhanced Visual Interfaces"; Kräutli, "Visualising Cultural Data"; Anne Bahde, "Conceptual Data Visualization in Archival Finding Aids: Preliminary User Responses," *portal: Libraries and the Academy* 17, no. 3 (2017): 485–506; A. Miller, "Data Visualization as Participatory Research: A Model for Digital Collections to Inspire User-Driven Research,"

Journal of Web Librarianship 13, no. 2 (2019): 127–77, https://doi.org/10.1080/19322909.2019.1586617.

27. Shiri, "Metadata-Enhanced Visual Interfaces"; Weijia Xu, Maria Esteva, Suyog Dutt Jain, and Varun Jain, "Analysis of Large Digital Collections with Interactive Visualization," in *2011 IEEE Conference on Visual Analytics Science and Technology (VAST)* (New York: IEEE, 2011), 241–50, https://doi.org/10.1109/VAST.2011.6102462; Kräutli, "Visualising Cultural Data."
28. Richard W. Hamming, *Numerical Methods for Scientists and Engineers* (New York: McGraw-Hill, 1962), vii, 276, 395.
29. Darrell Huff, *How to Lie with Statistics* (New York: W. W. Norton, 1954); Ray Lyons, "Beauty Is as Beauty Does," *Lib(rary) Performance* (blog), October 28, 2011, https://libperform.wordpress.com/2011/10/28/beauty-is-as-beauty-does/.
30. Richie Cotton, "Data Visualization for Everyone: An Introduction to Data Visualization with No Coding Involved," course on DataCamp platform, accessed June 26, 2020, https://learn.datacamp.com/courses/data-visualization-for-everyone (requires sign in).
31. Davis, Vane, and Kräutli, "Using Data Visualisation"; Kräutli, "Visualising Cultural Data."
32. Kräutli, "Visualising Cultural Data."
33. H. Porter Abbott, *The Cambridge Introduction to Narrative*, 2nd ed. (Cambridge: Cambridge University Press, 2008).
34. Edward Segel and Jeffrey Heer, "Narrative Visualization: Telling Stories with Data," *IEEE Transactions on Visualization and Computer Graphics* 16, no. 6 (2010), http://vis.stanford.edu/papers/narrative.
35. Wita Wojtkowski and W. Gregory Wojtkowski, "Storytelling: Its Role in Information Visualization" (paper, European Systems Science Congress, Crete, Greece, October 16–19, 2002), http://citeseerx.ist.psu.edu/viewdoc/citations;jsessionid=84B03925EA0F41B00DA79F9EE03F5932?doi=10.1.1.99.4771.
36. Yea-Seul Kim, Katharina Reinecke, and Jessica Hullman, "Explaining the Gap: Visualizing One's Predictions Improves Recall and Comprehension of Data," in *CHI '17: Proceedings of the 2017 CHI Conference on Human Factors in Computing Systems* (New York: Association for Computing Machinery, 2017), 1375–86, https://doi.org/10.1145/3025453.3025592.
37. Deal, "Visualizing Digital Collections"; Windhager et al., "A Review of Information Visualization Approaches"; Whitelaw, "Towards Generous Interfaces."
38. "Introducing GLAM Labs," in M. Mahey, A. Al-Abdulla, S. Ames, P. Bray, G. Candela, S. Chambers, C. Derven, et al., *Open a GLAM Lab* (Doha, Qatar: Qatar University Press, 2019), 33–45, https://glamlabs.pubpub.org/pub/kly6t0jq.
39. Europeana Pro home page, accessed May 12, 2020, https://pro.europeana.eu/; "Digital Scholarship," British Library, accessed June 2, 2020, https://www.bl.uk/subjects/digital-scholarship; "LC Labs," Library of Congress, accessed June 2, 2020, https://labs.loc.gov/; "DPLA Pro," Digital Public Library of America, accessed May 29, 2020, https://pro.dp.la/.
40. Burdick et al., *Digital Humanities*; Drucker, "5b. Data Mining and Text Analysis."
41. Burdick et al., *Digital Humanities*, 18.
42. Jessica Wagner Webster, "Digital Collaborations: A Survey Analysis of Digital Humanities Partnerships between Librarians and Other Academics," *DHQ: Digital Humanities Quarterly* 13, no. 4 (2019), http://www.digitalhumanities.org/dhq/vol/13/4/000441/000441.html.
43. OpenRefine home page, accessed May 24, 2020, https://openrefine.org/.
44. Phettelace, "Effectively Visualizing Library Data"; Deal, "Visualizing Digital Collections"; Finch and Flenner, "Using Data Visualization"; Chen, "Information Visualization"; Harris and Harris, "Data Visualization Tools."

## Chapter 2

Getting Started with R

R is now one of the most popular programming languages used by data scientists.[1] Supported by the not-for-profit R Foundation for Statistical Computing, R is free software under GNU General Public License copyleft, meaning that users can study, run, copy, distribute, and change it freely.[2] It is a system developed specifically for data analysis and graphics. R was designed originally by Ross Ihaka and Robert Gentleman at the Department of Statistics of the University of Auckland, New Zealand, in the early 1990s.[3] Its design was influenced by two other programming languages: the S programming language and the Scheme. Since mid-1997, the R Development Core Team, along with a well-established community of enthusiasts and supporters, has been advancing the R source code. This worldwide community of R coders has been meeting together annually at conferences called useR! since May 2004.

R's home page hosts all details on the R Project and the R Foundation, including a link to the Comprehensive R Archive Network (CRAN), help pages, and extensive documentation with a bibliography. R also has its own open access, refereed online periodical, *The R Journal,* published by the R Foundation in Vienna, Austria.[4] The journal focuses on R implementations, its applications, new packages, original features, and the latest releases. It also includes information about conferences related to R.

R home page
https://www.r-project.org/

R is relatively easy to learn, and it has 10,000 available packages, also called libraries, which perform sophisticated functions, such as statistics and visualizations, that do not need to be coded from scratch. This is one of the most compelling features of the R environment. Also, R is available via several interfaces, including command line, Jupyter notebook, and RStudio.[5]

Installing R

To install R, follow these steps:

1. Start with opening R Project in your browser: https://www.r-project.org/.
2. Go to the CRAN web page listed under Download: https://cran.r-project.org/mirrors.html.
   - CRAN displays mirror servers, organized by countries, that are used to distribute R code and packages. Instead of choosing a mirror that is near you, click on the first listed mirror, 0-Cloud, which automatically selects your location.
3. Choose an appropriate installation version for your operating system either Linux, macOs, or Windows.
4. Follow the installation steps.

The CRAN web pages include resources on the installation process under R Basics in the section Frequently Asked Questions on R.

Frequently Asked Questions on R: R Basics
https://cran.r-project.org/doc/FAQ/R-FAQ.html#R-Basics

Also, you will find more information on setting up R in the RStudio IDE (discussed below) under the Help and Tutorial tabs.

Plan on updating your R system regularly. A new version of R is released annually. Upgrading to the latest version involves reinstalling all packages.

Introducing RStudio

RStudio is one of the graphical interfaces for the R programming language. It is an integrated development environment (IDE) for R created by the software company RStudio PBC, founded by Joseph J. Allaire in 2009. The RStudio IDE supports writing scripts for data analysis, interactive web applications, documents, reports, and graphs. RStudio is available in open source and commercial editions, and it runs on all operating systems, including Windows, macOS, and Linux. It also has two formats: a desktop application and a server that allows working with RStudio through a web browser.

Installing RStudio

To install RStudio, follow these steps:

1. Make sure that R is already installed on your computer.
2. Go to the Download RStudio page: https://rstudio.com/products/rstudio/download/. This page can also be reached from the RStudio home page (https://rstudio.com) by selecting Products, then RStudio (under Open Source).
3. Select the RStudio Desktop free version with an open source license.
4. Follow the installation steps.
5. Pin the RStudio icon to your taskbar so you can find it easily.

Again, plan on upgrading your RStudio on a regular basis to take advantage of new packages and features. RStudio is updated every few months.

Getting Familiar with the RStudio IDE

Once you install RStudio, you can open it and get familiar with its structure and features. Figure 2.1 is a screenshot of the RStudio window with a visualization project in session. The window consists of the menu and four panes that can be rearranged depending on your particular needs: (1) the R Console pane, located in the lower left corner of the figure, (2) the Source Editor pane, above the R Console pane, (3) the Environment and History pane, in the upper right corner of the figure, and (4) the Miscellaneous pane, in the lower right corner of the figure.

The menu provides several drop-down menus and buttons for opening, examining, editing, and saving scripts and data. Here is a selection of functionalities needed for a basic workflow:

- File: create or open a file, create or open a project, save data, print, close a file or project, quit session
- Edit: undo/redo, copy and paste, search for text, clear console
- Code: insert code sections, run code, get help with applying functions
- View: zoom, move around tabs, view script and data
- Plots: navigate through plots, save plots, remove plots

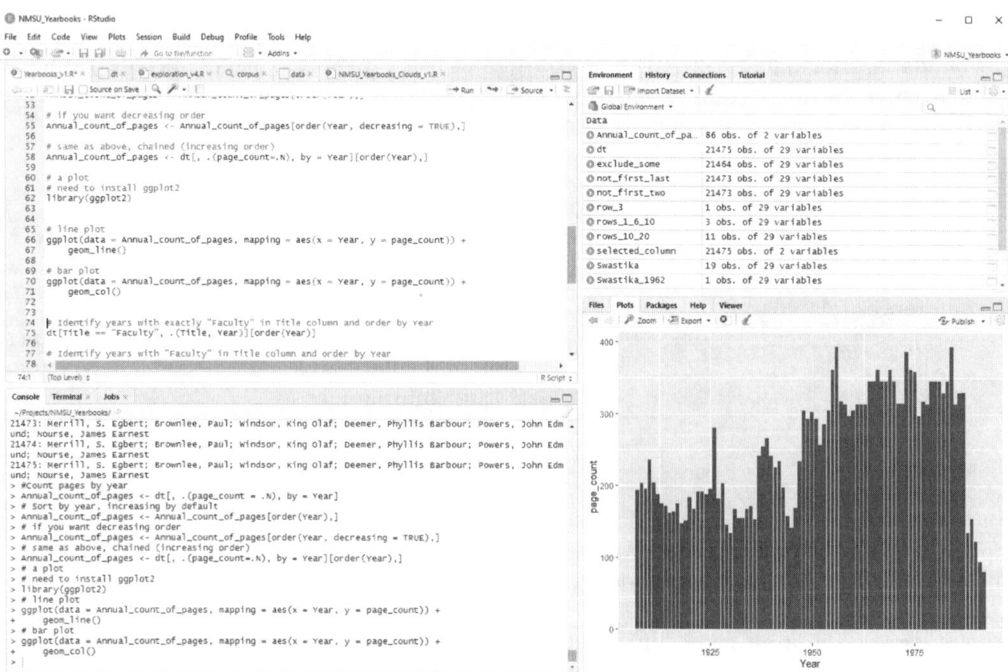

Figure 2.1
RStudio integrated development environment (IDE)

- Session: restart the R session, clear the workspace, set the working directory, save the R session
- Build/Debug/Profile: advanced tools for coding
- Tools: install packages, check for package updates
- Help: quick references, cheat sheets, links to RStudio documentation on products and services

The four panes in RStudio environment are designed to serve specific purposes:

1. The R Console pane is where you execute R commands interactively. The console allows the user to type commands directly following the flashing cursor, and then it displays the output for a given command, along with possible warnings and error messages. The Terminal tab next to the Console tab can be used to run shell commands directly in R.
2. The Source Editor pane is also for typing R scripts, but it supports many other programming languages as well. It is a comprehensive editing surface that provides snippets, built-in help, and autocompletion. In Source Editor, you can either execute a single line by selecting it with the cursor and then clicking on the Run button, or you can highlight a selection of the script's rows and then click on the Run button. The Source Editor pane also serves as an area where the data are displayed in spreadsheet form.
3. The Environment and History pane displays all of the data that are loaded during a session. This makes it easy to examine and save the data. To take a closer look at the data, click on a variable name, and the data will be shown in the Source Editor pane as a table. Other kinds of objects, such as variables and functions, can be inspected here as well. All previous commands are saved under the History tab, and they are easy to search and re-execute. The Git tab keeps track of your script versions. You can see the status of current files and sync them with files of other collaborators. Under the Connections tab, there is an area that allows connecting to databases, such as relational database SQL, and distributed tools, such as Apache Spark. The Tutorial tab provides fundamentals on data, observations, variables, and setting up R and RStudio.
4. The Miscellaneous pane consists of five tabs: Files, Plots, Packages, Help, and Viewer. The Files tab shows the content of your working directory. When R code uses plots, you can see them under the Plots tab. You can install, upgrade, and manage the R packages library under the Packages tab. An R package usually includes code, data, and documentation for the package and its associated functions. The Help tab is preloaded with all R language and RStudio documentation, including online learning resources, manuals, references, news, and technical specifications (see figure 2.2). The Viewer tab shows HTML output created with R Markdown and R Shiny packages.

It is a good practice to start working in RStudio by creating a new project (File → New Project). RStudio projects make it possible to keep independent pieces of your work in separate folders, with their own scripts, workspaces, and histories. One of the first R projects you may work on is replicating training sessions from online courses.

Also, be aware of objects in your workspace. It is good to clear your workspace when you need a fresh start while working on your project. Experts recommend frequently saving your projects, scripts, and data, rather than your workspace.[6]

Learning R at DataCamp

There are multiple online courses and tutorials on R and RStudio. Coursera, edX, Udacity, Codecademy, and Udemy are just a few popular educational platforms offering numerous courses on the R programming language and its applications. For the purpose of creating basic visualizations for digital collections, I chose to learn R at DataCamp. Conveniently, DataCamp provides short lessons that can fit within the time constraints of a busy schedule. Each lesson consists of a brief video lecture and hands-on interactive exercises done in an environment resembling RStudio. The screenshot in figure 2.3 shows the DataCamp environment.

Thus far, I have completed four courses: Data Visualization for Everyone with Richie Cotton, Introduction to R with Jonathan Cornelissen, Data Manipulation with data.table in R with Matt Dowle (the author of the data.table package) and Arun Srinivasan, and

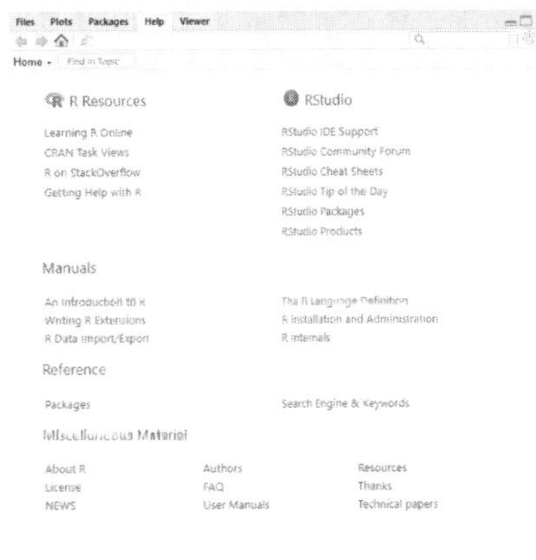

Figure 2.2
RStudio Help tab resources

Data Visualization with ggplot2 (Part1) with Rick Scavetta.[7] With no background in computer programming, I was able to create basic visualizations for the Tombaugh Papers digital collection based on what I learned during these introductory courses. R truly is for everyone. And as you see below, learning it is a matter of several hours. Some of the training data sets, such as *iris* and *mtcars*, used in DataCamp classes are available in R. They load automatically with each new R session. I would recommend repeating the exercises in RStudio to get a better feel for this new work environment and also to be open to taking risks, making mistakes, and experimenting. This is the best mindset for learning a new language and its culture.

There are multiple online courses and tutorials on R and RStudio. Here are just a few popular educational platforms offering numerous courses on R programming language and its applications.

Codecademy
https://www.codecademy.com/

Coursera
https://www.coursera.org/

DataCamp
https://www.datacamp.com/

edX
https://www.edx.org/

Udacity
https://www.udacity.com/

Udemy
https://www.udemy.com/

General Workflow of Visualization

Once you have all of the pieces of software installed and tested with standard, public data sets (for example, *iris* and *mtcars*) and are developing some understanding of how to use them effectively, you may begin experimenting with your own data. I exported the whole collection data from CONTENTdm, a digital content management system, as a tab-delimited text file. I saved it in a subfolder titled *data* in the R project folder. This way, instead of providing the full path to the data set in a file reading function, it was enough to put just a relative path to **`data subfolder`** to upload the data set to RStudio, as shown below:

```
fread("data/Tombaugh_Export_LTR.txt")
```

Listed below are the stages of the visualization process.

1. The very first step is installing needed packages for specific visualizations. It can be done in two different ways:

   a. Click on the Packages tab in the Miscellaneous pane and select the needed packages to install. The autocomplete feature will help you find the right packages (figure 2.4).
   b. You can also manually install packages in the console by using **`install.packages()`** function as shown below:

```
install.packages("data.table")
```

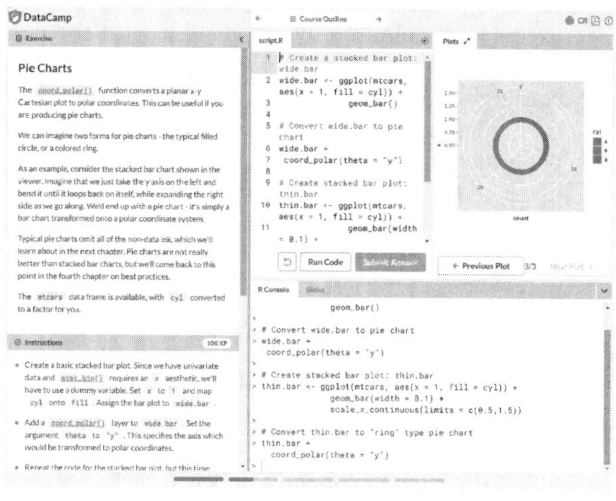

Figure 2.3
DataCamp learning environment

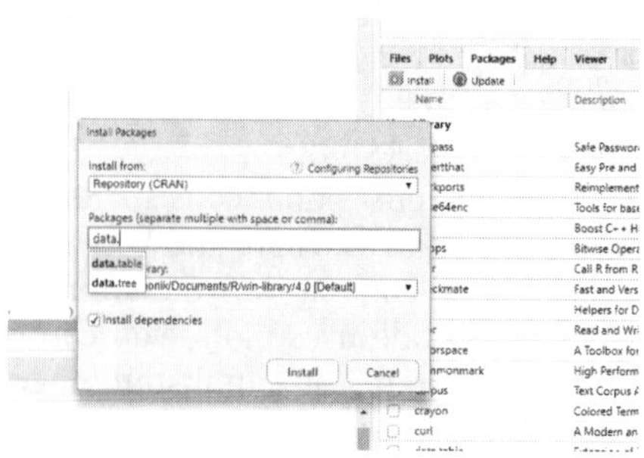

Figure 2.4
RStudio installing R packages option

2. The next step is loading the needed packages to the workspace during a given session. Load the packages each time a new session is started. In order to do so, use the function **library()**:

```
library(data.table)
library(ggplot2)
```

3. Now, it is time to load a data set into a workspace as a data table. For this purpose, use the function **fread()** that comes with the data.table package. Call the **fread()** function with the path to your data file (tab-delimited or comma-separated) as an argument, as presented below:

```
data <- fread("data/Tombaugh_Export_
LTR.txt")
```

4. After loading your data set, it is a good idea to carefully examine the data. The assumption here is that the data set is already well structured and clear of most issues, such as errors, inconsistencies, typos, and missing values.

   However, it is a good practice to double-check the data for problems that may impair their visualization. For example, if while examining the data, you happen to spot some missing values but there are not many of them, you can exclude rows with missing values without affecting the graph accuracy.

   Oftentimes, some problems with data can be discovered while producing graphs. For instance, when creating the bar plot for the Tombaugh Papers digital collection that was to show counts of documents in individual series of professional papers, we discovered that a big chunk of the documents from the New Mexico State University series carried a typo: "Sate" instead of "State." This mistake had a serious impact on the histogram showing the distribution of documents across different series. It is worth keeping in mind that by nature, all data and metadata tend to be messy. Finding a problem should not be a surprise. After identifying issues, you fix it and then move on. There are many tools to help with cleaning data, including OpenRefine, mentioned in chapter 1, and R.[8]
5. Depending on the question you want to address with a specific type of visualization, you may need to preprocess your data. Sometimes, preprocessing might involve selecting rows from a given time interval—for example, the 1940s—or from a given category—for instance, the Lowell Observatory correspondence series. It might also involve calculating various measures (such as document counts or mean and median values) over data aggregated by time units, categories, and so on. Specific examples of preprocessing data will be presented in chapter 3.
6. The final step involves calling specific plotting functions from the ggplot2 package and tuning plots for more effective communication and an appealing look.

Essential R Packages for Visualizations

Three fundamental packages used in all our visualizations are data.table, created by Matt Dowle, and ggplot2 and tidyr, both designed by Hadley Wickham.[9] The data.table package represents a spreadsheet with variables in columns and observations in rows. It is a modified version of data.frame, optimized for run time and memory efficiency. In the context of digital collection, we can use data.table to examine data sets, to manipulate and transform data, and to produce input for visualizations. Below is a brief overview of the data.table syntax.

The general form of data.table syntax consists of three components: *i*, *j*, and *by*:

```
DT[i, j, by]
```

In *i*, you can filter rows.

In *j*, you can define manipulation of columns, such as selecting, applying functions to, dropping, or adding.

In *by*, you can define groupings of rows based on unique values in specified grouping columns.

An example of filtering rows done in the *i* component is as follows. In the case of the Tombaugh Papers digital collection data, in order to obtain only the family correspondence from the collection, we filtered rows where the values in "Series" column were equal to "Family Correspondence":

```
family_correspondence <- data[Series ==
"Family Correspondence",]
```

Note that the symbol **<-** is equivalent to **=**, an assignment operation.

An example of computation on grouped data while using components *j* and *by* is producing annual counts of documents in the collection:

```
annual_counts <- data[, .(count=.N),
by=year]
```

Starting from the left, we assigned the result of the operation to data table "annual_counts." In the *j* component, we created a new column, "count," and assigned to it the number of rows, represented by **.N**. In the *by* component, rows were grouped by unique values in the column "year." As a result, a number of rows per year was generated and stored in the "annual_counts" data table in the column "count."

The package ggplot2 is used to create graphic representations of data. It implements the concept of layered grammar of graphics originally formulated by Leland Wilkinson.[10] Each layer contributes to creating the objects that you see on the plot, and it shows a different aspect of the data set. The first four basic layers embedded inside the R programming language include data, aesthetics, geometries, and facet specifications. A data layer refers to the concrete set of variables that is plotted. An aesthetics layer refers to the scales onto which you map the concrete data set. For instance, you might map "time" to the horizontal (*x*) axis and "count" to the vertical (*y*) axis. An aesthetics layer also controls fill, color, labels size, shapes, and line types. A Geometries layer manages the type of plot that you employ. For example, **`geom_point()`** creates a scatter plot, **`geom_histogram()`** creates a histogram, **`geom_bar()`** creates a bar plot, and **`geom_line()`** creates a line plot.

A Facets layer controls creating subplots—separate displays—for each subset of the data. For instance, **`facet_grid()`** forms a matrix of panels defined by variables from rows and columns, while **`facet_wrap()`** creates a list of panels defined by a single variable.

The concept of tidying data refers to cleaning and structuring data in order to facilitate their visualization and analysis.[11] Tidy data sets have a clear structure where each variable is a column and each observation is a row. The package tidyr is used to transform data into a tidy format.

Choosing Plot Types

It is worth keeping in mind that current visualization techniques have their own legacy from business applications and governmental and administrative organizations, as well as from natural and social sciences since the eighteenth century.[12] Common charts, graphs, and diagrams have long been used by businessmen, administrators, and scientists to summarize quantitative information and translate it into graphic formats for a better grasp. Visualization has been both an analytical tool for exploring data and a communication tool for informing and persuading. While graphs illustrate data and may show their hidden patterns, they might also supply an interpretation of data. Choosing the right plot for your data may help to convey the right message.

In principle, plots are used to show patterns and trends in data. Andrew Abela created a typology of charts organized along four fundamental purposes for visualization, namely, comparison, distribution, composition, and relationship.[13] His typology provides a good starting point for selecting plots that may fit a particular task relevant for visualizing digital collection data:

- To compare variables, bar plots, dot plots, and line plots seem to be good choices.
    - Bar plots present the relationships between categoric and numeric variables.
    - Dot plots show a numeric metric for each category.
    - Line plots display the evolution of numeric variables.
- To show a distribution of data, you can employ bar and line histograms, box plots, and rose plots.
    - Histograms show the frequency of numeric variables.
    - Box plots summarize the distributions of numeric variables with median and quartiles.
    - Rose plots show the cyclical distribution.
- To determine the composition of data, you may use stacked bar plots, stacked area plots, pie charts, and tree maps.
    - Stacked bar charts show variations among many variables.
    - Stacked area charts present multiple variables changing over an interval.
    - Pie charts show numerical proportions among subsets of data.
    - Tree maps display tree-structured hierarchical data as a set of nested rectangles.
- To explore relationships among variables, you may use scatter plots, bubble plots, and heat maps.
    - Scatter plots reveal correlations between two numeric variables.
    - Bubble plots show patterns and correlations among multiple numeric variables.
    - Heat maps display a general view of multiple variables through color variations.

There are numerous resources that may guide you in selecting the best plot for your needs. For example, The Data Visualisation Catalogue, developed by Severino Ribecca, provides an extensive selection of diagrams, graphs, charts, and maps organized by multiple data visualization functions. Similarly, The Visualization Universe, a project developed by Anna and Mark Vital from Adioma Infographic Labs and Aleksander Vushkan in collaboration with Google News Lab, offers brief introductions to over fifty-five charts, along with a comprehensive list of books on data visualization and specialized tools. Likewise, Chartopedia, created

The following is a sample of possible questions about a digital collection's content that can be answered with various graphs.

1. What is the composition of the collection?

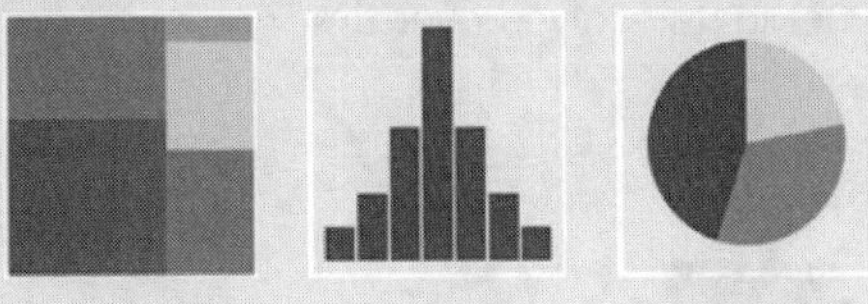

Figure 2.5
Tree map, histogram, and pie chart

2. How has the composition changed over time?

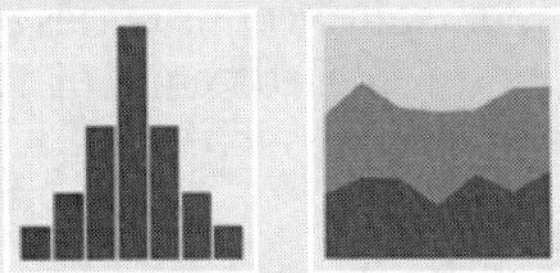

Figure 2.6
Histogram and stacked area 100% chart

3. How do the volumes of document series change over time?

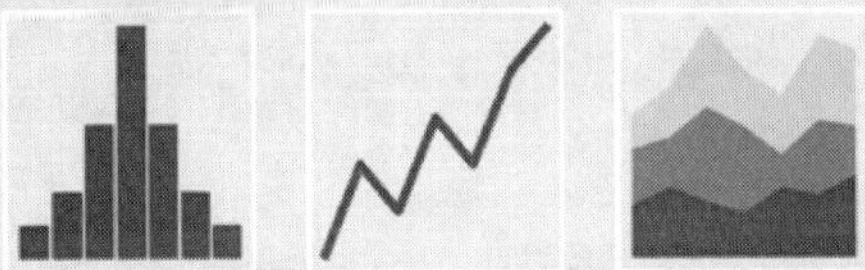

Figure 2.7
Histogram, line plot and stacked area chart

4. What is the time correlation between volumes of document series?

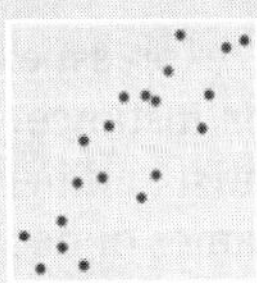

Figure 2.8
Scatter plot

5. What is the distribution of document counts among the creators of documents?

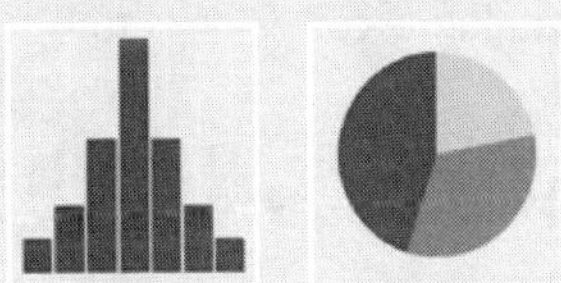

Figure 2.9
Histogram and pie chart

6. What is the distribution of document counts among the creators of documents and across series?

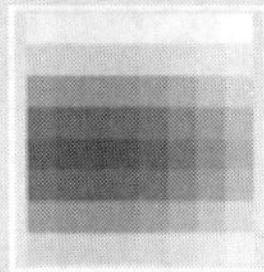

Figure 2.10
Heat map

7. What is the distribution of types of records in a collection?

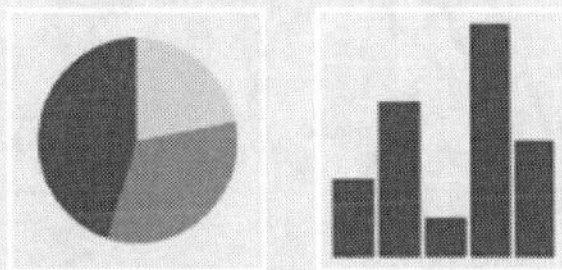

Figure 2.11
Pie chart and bar chart

8. What are frequencies of specific terms in a given collection?

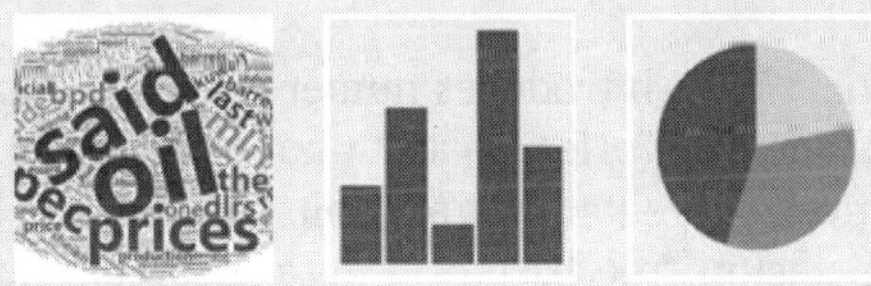

Figure 2.12
Word cloud, bar chart, and pie chart

9. Where or from whom do the collection documents come?

Figure 2.13
Map

10. How has collection developed over time?

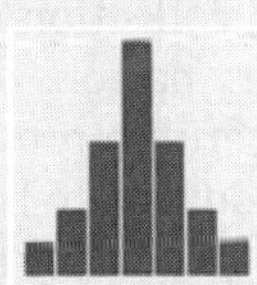

Figure 2.14
Histogram

The following is a sample of possible questions about a digital collection's content that can be answered with various graphs.

11. What terms from controlled vocabularies are the most frequently used?

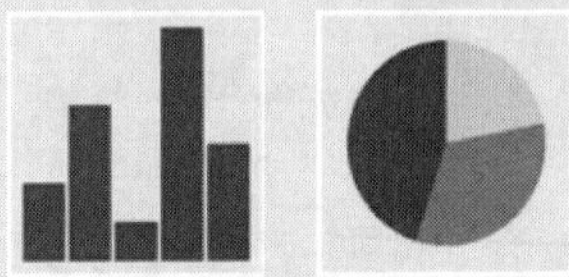

Figure 2.15
Bar chart and pie chart

12. How have controlled vocabularies evolved?

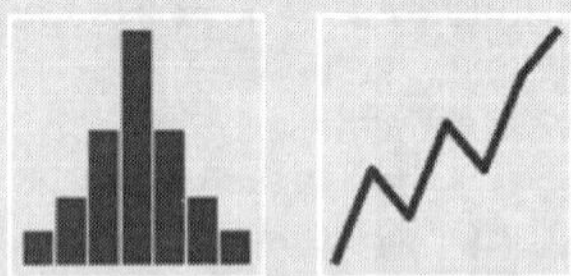

Figure 2.16
Histogram and line plot

13. How has the frequency of missing values in metadata evolved over time?

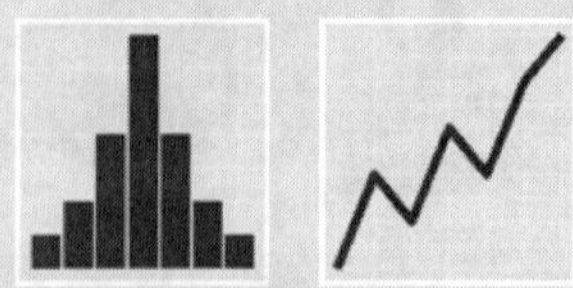

Figure 2.17
Histogram and line plot

14. What common metadata inconsistencies are detectable in graphs (misspelled names of categories: authors, series names, etc.)?

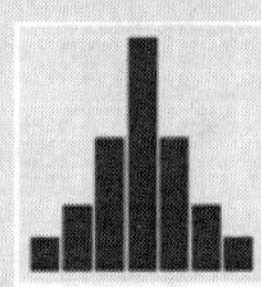

Figure 2.18
Histogram

by AnyChart LLC, introduces numerous chart types in various usage categories. Last but not least, From Data to Viz, a project created by Yan Holts and Conor Healy, offers a decision tree based on data formats and recommends various graphic possibilities for representing the formats. In addition to an overview of graph types, the site provides tips on using graphs along with the code for creating plots in a few programming languages, including R, Python, and D3.js. As I mentioned earlier, data visualization is a rapidly developing field that provides a wide range of resources and support to novices and experts alike. It is just a matter of taking on this new and exciting challenge.

What to Visualize

What to visualize depends on a combination of various elements. First, consider the content of a collection and think about what aspects of the collection could be of interest to its users, either library patrons or collection curators. For example, is it useful to provide a visual overview of the collection in addition to having a written description on the collection's landing page? Can visuals reveal patterns and details about the collection that otherwise would remain hidden? Would visual interactive features provide additional insights into the collection?

Another consideration involves examining a collection's data along with associated metadata in order to assess whether the information that you seek to visualize can indeed be extracted from the data. For example, can you show a network of professional relationships of a scientist based on the information contained in his papers?

The final concern is how to express extracted information in a graphic form. For instance, do you draw a network diagram for a scientist and her professional relationships based on the names of people that

There are numerous resources that may guide you in selecting the best plot for your needs.

The Data Visualisation Catalogue
https://datavizcatalogue.com/index.html

The Visualization Universe
http://visualizationuniverse.com/

Chartopedia
https://www.anychart.com/chartopedia

From Data to Viz
https://www.data-to-viz.com/

she corresponded with? Or perhaps you can use the information from envelopes about locations that letters were sent from and draw a map.

In selecting possible topics for visualizations that are to enhance your digital collections, it is important to know the limits of your data and metadata. But this knowledge should not stop you from experimenting with data. On the contrary, the process that leads to visualizations is exploratory in its very nature. Good and bad charts equally provide a lot of information about your data and metadata that you can use to improve your collections and make them more useful and appealing to library users.

The next chapter focuses on visualizations created for the NMSU Department of Astronomy's Clyde W. Tombaugh Papers digital collection hosted at the NMSU Library. The selection of graphs was informed by specific questions about the collection content and its development.

Notes

1. "TIOBE Programming Community Index for July 2020," accessed July 6, 2020, https://www.tiobe.com/tiobe-index/ (July 2020 information removed from page). TIOBE is a measure of popularity of a given programming language.
2. "What Is Free Software?" GNU Operating System, accessed July 6, 2020, https://www.gnu.org/philosophy/free-sw.html.
3. Kurt Hornik, "2.1 What Is R?" in "Frequently Asked Questions on R, Version 2020-02-20," accessed July 6, 2020, https://cran.r-project.org/doc/FAQ/R-FAQ.html#What-is-R_003f.
4. R Journal home page, accessed July 6, 2020, https://journal.r-project.org/.
5. Jupyter home page, accessed July 7, 2020, https://jupyter.org/; RStudio home page, accessed July 7, 2020, https://rstudio.com/.
6. J. D. Long and Paul Teetor, *R Cookbook: Proven Recipes for Data Analysis, Statistics and Graphics* (Sebastopol, CA: O'Reilly Media, 2019), 10–11.
7. Richie Cotton, "Data Visualization for Everyone," course on DataCamp platform, accessed December 2019, https://learn.datacamp.com/courses/data-visualization-for-everyone (requires sign-in); Jonathan Cornelissen, "Introduction to R," course on DataCamp platform, accessed November 2019, https://learn.datacamp.com/courses/free-introduction-to-r (requires sign-in); Matt Dowle, "Data Manipulation with data.table in R," course on DataCamp platform, accessed January 2020, https://learn.datacamp.com/courses/data-manipulation-with-datatable-in-r (requires sign-in); Rick Scavetta, "Data Visualization with ggplot2 (Part 1)," course on DataCamp platform, accessed December 2019, https://learn.datacamp.com/courses/data-visualization-with-ggplot2-1 (requires sign-in).
8. OpenRefine home page, accessed June 14, 2020, https://openrefine.org/; Edwin de Jonge and Mark van der Loo, *An Introduction to Data Cleaning with R*, discussion paper (The Hague: Statistics Netherlands, 2013), https://cran.r-project.org/doc/contrib/de_Jonge+van_der_Loo-Introduction_to_data_cleaning_with_R.pdf.
9. Hadley Wickham, "A Layered Grammar of Graphics," *Journal of Computational and Graphical Statistics* 19, no. 1 (2010): 3–28; Hadley Wickham, "Tidy Data," *Journal of Statistical Software* 59 (2014), https://vita.had.co.nz/papers/tidy-data.html.
10. Leland Wilkinson, *Grammar of Graphics*, 2nd ed. (New York: Springer, 2005).
11. Wickham, "Tidy Data."
12. Anne Burdick, Johanna Drucker, Peter Lunenfeld, Todd Presner and Jeffrey Schnapp, *Digital Humanities* (Cambridge, MA: MIT Press, 2012); Daniel Rosenberg and Anthony Grafton, *Cartographies of Time: A History of the Timeline* (New York: Princeton Architectural Press, 2010).
13. Andrew Abela, *Advanced Presentation by Design: Creating Communication That Drives Action*, 2nd ed. (San Francisco: Pfeiffer, 2013); Andrew Abela, The Extreme Presentation Method (website), accessed June 20, 2020, https://extremepresentation.com/.

## Chapter 3

Visualizations of a Digital Collection's Data

This chapter presents an extended example of visualizing the digital collection of papers of the astronomer Clyde W. Tombaugh (1906–1997) at New Mexico State University Library Archives and Special Collections. A series of R plots offers insight into Tombaugh's professional and personal life as revealed through his papers, as well as into the administrative side of managing the collection.

About Clyde W. Tombaugh

Clyde William Tombaugh was an American planetary astronomer who discovered the ninth planet in our solar system, Pluto, when he was twenty-four years old. His story is quite incredible. He was a farm boy in Kansas who liked to join his father and uncle when they stargazed in their spare time. Both men readily shared with Clyde what they learned during their informal studies and practice. The boy got inspired and constructed several telescopes with parts of discarded farm machinery. He began exploring the night skies on his own. Young Clyde was fascinated with Mars and Jupiter. When he sent his sketches of these planets to the Lowell Observatory at Flagstaff, Arizona, in 1929 asking for some feedback, its director V. M. Slipher offered him a job as a technician.

At the time, a new telescope at the Lowell Observatory had just been completed, and Tombaugh was hired to renew the photographic search for trans-Neptunian planet X. The mysterious planet X had been postulated by Percival Lowell, the founder of the observatory, in 1905. Tombaugh found planet X on February 18, 1930, a year after he was hired. He was the only American astronomer who found a planet in our solar system.[1] The discovery was announced almost a month later, on March 13—Percival Lowell's birthday and the date of the discovery of Uranus by William Herschel in 1781. In recognition of his spectacular achievement in observational astronomy, Tombaugh was awarded the Jackson Gwilt Medal and Gift by the British Royal Astronomical Society.[2] In February and March 2020, the Lowell Observatory, along with New Mexico State University, celebrated the ninetieth anniversary of this incredible discovery by a young man who reached the stars.[3]

For Tombaugh, the discovery of Pluto was just the beginning of an exciting career. Awarded the Edwin Emory Slosson Scholarship to the University of Kansas, he pursued his education and earned bachelor's and master's degrees in astronomy in 1936 and 1939 respectively. In the meantime, he was still engaged in research projects at the Lowell Observatory. While working in Flagstaff, he discovered multiple clusters and superclusters of galaxies, clusters of stars, asteroids, and comets. He also fully explored what he called the Great Perseus-Andromeda Stratum of Extra-galactic Nebulae.[4]

During World War II, Tombaugh taught physics at Arizona State Teachers College and then navigation for the V-12 Navy program. In the following academic year, 1945–46, he worked for the astronomy department at the University of California at Los Angeles (UCLA), teaching both astronomy and the history of astronomy. He then moved to Las Cruces, New Mexico, where he was hired as chief of the optical measurements section at the ballistic research laboratory at the White Sands Proving Ground, and then as an optical physicist at its systems engineering branch. Tombaugh's work there focused on German V-2 rockets, obtained at the end of war, and included designing tracking telescopes used to photograph missiles and rockets.

Involved in rocketry research during the Cold War and the space race, Tombaugh also initiated extensive satellite searches, originally conducted at the Lowell Observatory, then moved to the White Sands Proving Ground, and eventually transferred to the Physical Science Laboratory at New Mexico State University (NMSU) in 1955. The satellite search project led

Tombaugh's group to the Quito Observatory in Ecuador, where the photographs of the Russian *Sputnik I* were taken. No other small natural, near-Earth satellites were discovered. Tombaugh's final report for NASA provided solid evidence for carrying out safe space exploration.

Tombaugh also initiated a photographic Planetary Patrol and Study Project of five planets: Mercury, Venus, Mars, Jupiter, and Saturn. The patrol was conducted from 1958 to 1973, mainly at the NMSU Research Center, where Tombaugh began working as an associate research professor in 1959. A year later, in recognition of his contributions to space sciences, he was awarded an honorary doctorate by Northern Arizona University. While at NMSU, Tombaugh returned to his earliest fascination and focused his research on Mars and its geology.

Tombaugh (figure 3.1) was one of the founding members of the department of astronomy at NMSU, where he taught until his retirement in 1973. During his tenure he also contributed to the establishment of the planetary observatory on the campus and the graduate program in astronomy.

In 1980, the fiftieth anniversary of the Pluto discovery, Tombaugh published his discovery account entitled *Out of Darkness: The Planet Pluto*, which he coauthored with Patrick Moore. The same year, he was inducted into the International Space Hall of Fame, established in 1976 at the New Mexico Museum of Space History in recognition of those who advanced human knowledge of the universe.[5] In 1986, the Clyde Tombaugh Scholars Fund was established to support young space scientists in the department of astronomy at NMSU.[6]

Tombaugh conducted astronomical research and kept using his own telescopes until the end of his life. He used to comment on his career that he really had a tour of the heavens.[7] Tombaugh died in 1997 in Mesilla Park, near Las Cruces, New Mexico. His ashes were placed inside *New Horizons*, an interplanetary space probe launched by NASA in 2006 to explore Jupiter, Pluto, and objects in the Kuiper Belt. The Tombaugh Regio, a large heart-shaped light-colored surface feature of Pluto, is named after him, as is the asteroid 1604 Tombaugh.

Figure 3.1
Professor Tombaugh working in his NMSU office

Clyde W. Tombaugh Papers Archival Collection

After Tombaugh's death, most of his papers were donated to the New Mexico State University Library Archives and Special Collections for preservation and access. One hundred thirty linear feet of materials without any original order were structured and organized into a manuscript collection added to the Rio Grande Historical Collections.[8]

Initially, Tombaugh's collection was divided broadly into personal and professional papers. These two categories were further organized into specific subseries, including extensive correspondence arranged either alphabetically by correspondent name or chronologically. Personal papers include documents related to Tombaugh's youth in Kansas and his early interest in optics, telescopes, and stargazing, as well as his education and first work experiences at the Lowell Observatory. This part of the collection also covers his family correspondence, his deep commitment to the Unitarian Universalist Church, celebrations of Pluto discovery anniversaries, and fan mail. Tombaugh was a well-regarded figure in astronomy circles worldwide, and he also was highly popular with the public. He received tens of thousands of letters from amateur astronomers, aspiring scholars, and schoolchildren from across the world. He kept most of them.

Tombaugh's professional papers were organized by the institutions he worked for: namely, the Lowell Observatory, Arizona State Teachers College, UCLA, the White Sands Proving Ground, and New Mexico State University. These papers include his voluminous correspondence with his fellow astronomers, astrophysicists, and other scientists and scholars from related fields, as well as his research reports and files, speeches and lectures, and writings. Several of his major projects are especially well documented in the collection, including the Near Earth Satellite Search, the Planetary Patrol and Study Project, and his lifelong studies on Mars, as well as his work on optics and construction of reflecting telescopes. The collection also includes firsthand accounts of his discovery of Pluto and subsequent research on it, which Tombaugh monitored closely over the years. The original photographic plates that Tombaugh used in his search for planet X, along with related documents, are held by the Lowell Observatory Archives in Flagstaff, Arizona.

In addition, the NMSU collection includes Tombaugh's photographs, technical reports, maps, and design drawings of tracking telescopes. In 2003

Herbert A. Beebe, Tombaugh's associate, donated to the collection a set of oral histories conducted with Tombaugh and his family, friends, and colleagues. These personal recollections of the past events, recorded in audio and video formats, added a final touch to this comprehensive collection.

The processing of the entire collection was completed in 2004. The finding aid, which thoroughly describes the scope, organization, and content of the collection, consists of 158 pages. This number directly speaks to the volume of the collection, which, in turn, reflects the productive life of a passion-driven scientist.

Clyde W. Tombaugh Papers Digital Collection

The digitization of Tombaugh's papers started in 2015 with a goal of providing online access to his legacy. The structure of the digital collection reflects the arrangement of the physical collection, with specific series, boxes, and folders containing related documents. This mirroring of the archival collection was made possible by using features for collecting and storing compound objects provided by OCLC's CONTENTdm platform. As a result, the organization and description of the digitized material are consistent with the description provided in the archival finding aid, which facilitates the work of researchers and students who use both collections.

Most of the series from the personal papers are already added to the online collection, as is a substantial part of the professional papers. In addition to text documents, the digital collection includes a number of photographs and a representative sample of various drawings that Tombaugh did of telescope designs, focusing devices, optical systems, satellites, planetary sketches, and constellation

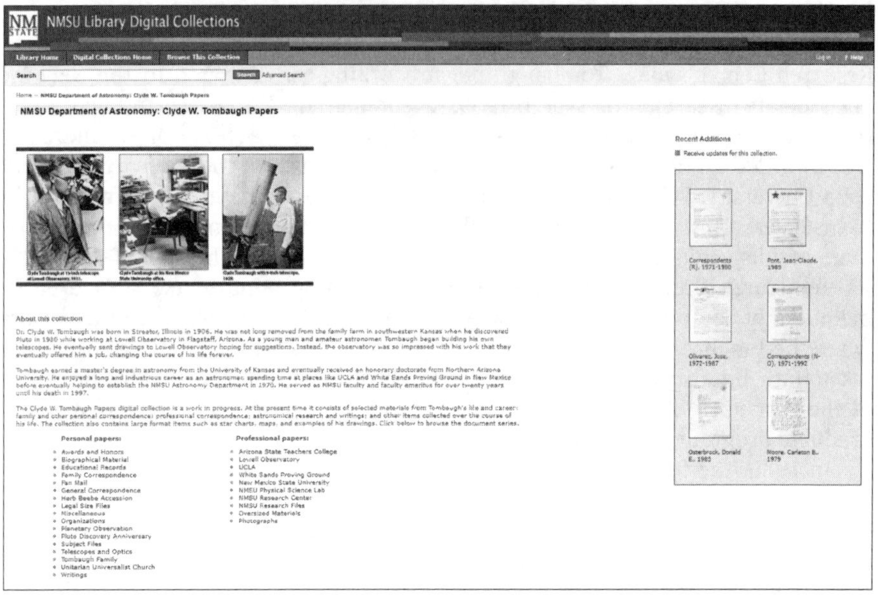

Figure 3.2
Tombaugh Papers digital collection's landing page

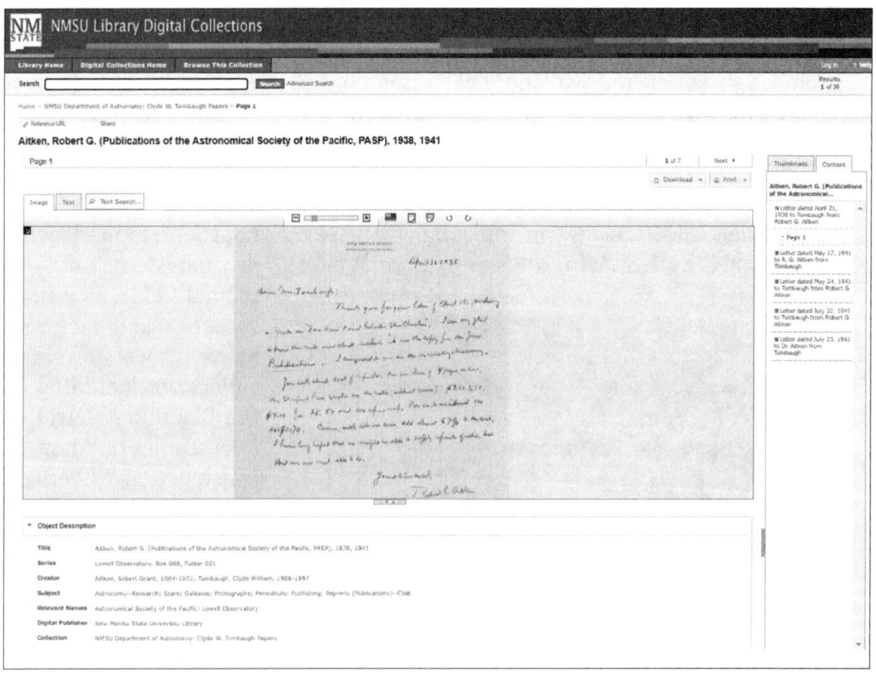

Figure 3.3
Tombaugh Papers digital collection—item view

charts. A screenshot of the landing page of the Tombaugh digital collection is shown in figure 3.2.

Photographs at the top of the landing page, along with a short description of the collection, are meant to provide quick insight into collection content and its historical context. In addition to a brief overview of Tombaugh's scientific career, the text introduces the status and progress made in the development of digital collection. Divided into two main categories, a list of links to various subseries allows a reader to get a sense of the materials included. It is impossible, however, to get an estimate of the collection's breadth and volume based on this brief introduction.

Similarly, neither browsing through the collection nor reading the metadata describing folders and individual pages of documents provides a comprehensive overview of the collection. Due to limitations of screen displays, one can examine only a few records at a time while browsing or just focus on a document page (see figure 3.3).

Visualizations of the collection content can remedy these shortcomings. By providing overviews of a collection, visualizations help a reader to see not just one page, but all pages at once.

In the next section, eighteen charts provide holistic views of the collection and offer some additional insights into its content that both library users and cataloguers may find valuable.

Selected Visualizations Created for the Clyde W. Tombaugh Papers Digital Collection

What follows are visualizations that address specific questions about the Tombaugh Papers digital collection. Each plot is described and interpreted briefly. Likewise, a script for each plot is presented and explained in some detail. The R code for a given plot is divided according to the stages of a basic workflow, that is: loading R packages, loading data, transforming data, and plotting. In addition, in order to demonstrate what sets of values are translated into graphic forms, relevant data tables or their fragments are included.

Please note that the scripts provided below can be replicated and used to create visualizations with different sets of data. The readers of this report are encouraged to use the information below and start experimenting with R.

Question 1: How Many Documents Were Created in Successive Years?

Plot 1 (figure 3.4) is a time line graph. It gives an overview of the collection at a glance. This plot is the first holistic view of the Tombaugh collection. One can see at once how many documents of all categories were produced in successive years between 1900 and 2000. Apparently, the 1950s are best represented in the collection. This is the time when Tombaugh worked at the White Sands Proving Ground and at New Mexico State University.

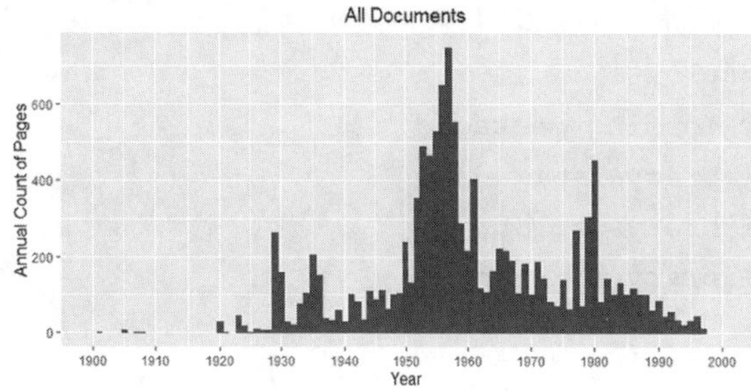

Figure 3.4
Plot 1—time line graph for all documents in the Tombaugh Papers digital collection

In order to create a plot, first load the needed packages by calling the function **library()**:

- **library(data.table)**—for data mining and processing
- **library(ggplot2)**—for data plotting
- **library(stringr)**—for string operations, such as detecting and extracting character patterns

Second, load the exported data into a data table called "data." This is done by using the function **fread()** included in the data.table package:

```
data <- fread("data/Tombaugh_Export_LTR.
txt")
```

Then change the original names of the columns. R does not accept column names with spaces. For this, use the function **setnames()**. Call the function **setnames()** with data and then for the original name, substitute a new name linking the words with an underscore:

```
setnames(data, "Date Original",
"date_original")
```

Next, use the function **setcolorder()** to change the order of the columns to see the one of interest up front in the table:

```
setcolorder(data, "date_original")
```

In the next line, extract the year from the string **date_original** and store it in the new column "year" as a numeric value. This operation is performed on all rows in the "date_original" column.

R SCRIPT FOR PLOT 1

```
# plot_1
# loading packages
library(data.table)
library(ggplot2)
library(stringr)

# loading data
data <- fread("data/Tombaugh_Export_LTR.txt")

# transforming data
setnames(data, "Date Original", "date_original")
setcolorder(data, "date_original")
data[, year := as.numeric(str_extract(date_original, "\\d{4}"))]
annual_counts <- na.omit(data[, .(annual_count = .N), by = year][order(year)])

# plotting
ggplot(data=annual_counts, aes(x = year, y = annual_count)) +
    geom_col(fill = "deeppink4", color = "deeppink4") +
    scale_x_continuous(breaks = seq(1900, 2000, by = 10),
                       limits = c(1900, 2000)) +
    labs(x = "Year", y = "Annual Count of Pages") +
    ggtitle("All Documents") +
    theme(plot.title = element_text(hjust = 0.5, size = 14),
          axis.title = element_text(size = 12))
```

The function **`str_extract()`**, which comes from the stringr library, is used here to extract a string representing year from the string in column "date_original." Using regular expressions,[9] this function looks for a pattern of four consecutive digits (using the expression **`"\\d{4}"`**). Then, the string representing the year is converted to a numeric value by another function, **`as.numeric()`**. Now, the numeric value gets assigned to a new column, called "year," created (in place) in the table "data" with the operator **`":="`**.

```
annual_counts_original <- na.omit(data[,
.(annual_count = .N), by = year]
[order(year)])
```

In the next step, produce annual counts of records for each year. Using the data.table syntax, create a new data table with two columns, "year" and "annual_count," the latter one filled with the number of all rows (**`.N`**) for each year (**`by = year`**):

```
data[, .(annual_count = .N), by = year].
```

This operation is then followed by ordering rows with the function **`order()`**, which sorts annual counts chronologically. All the records with missing dates are deselected by the function **`na.omit()`**. The result of all operations is then stored in the data table "annual_counts," which has two columns, "year" and "annual_count," as shown in table 3.1.

Table 3.1
Plot 1 data

year	annual_count
1895	1
1901	1
1905	7
1907	1
1908	1
1920	28

```
# plotting
ggplot(data=annual_counts, aes(x = year, y
= annual_count)) +
    geom_col(fill = "deeppink4", color =
    "deeppink4") +
    scale_x_continuous(breaks = seq(1900,
    2000, by = 10),
         limits = c(1900, 2000)) +
    labs(x = "Year", y = "Annual Count of
    Pages") +
    ggtitle("All Documents") +
    theme(plot.title = element_text(hjust
    = 0.5, size = 14),
         axis.title = element_text(size =
         12))
```

To produce a plot, call the **ggplot()** function with the data table "annual_counts" as **data**, and then within the same function define the *x* and *y* axes with the **aes()** function. For *x*, use the column "year," and for *y*, use the column "annual_count" defined before in the data table "annual_count_original."

In the next line, define the plot type. The **geom_col()** function stands for the bar plot with arguments **color** and **fill** specified by **"deeppink4"**. Note that the plus signs mean adding additional layers to the plot. In the next line, define the range of years for the *x* axis (1900 to 2000), and set tick spacing (**breaks**) to every ten years. Then, define labels for the *x* and *y* axes labels as "Year" and "Annual Count of Pages" respectively.

In the next step, define the title for the entire plot as "All Documents." The last line calls the function **theme()**, which sets the central position and the font size of the plot title. The **theme()** function can be used to define many other details of the plot, such as font sizes of axis text, axis tick intervals, and so on.

Question 2: How Do the Volumes of Personal and Professional Correspondence Compare?

Plot 2 (figure 3.5), a bar plot, also displays an overview of the collection at a glance. Bar plots are employed to show the relationship between numeric and categorical variables. This bar plot compares the volumes of two categories, personal and professional papers. At the current stage of collection development, personal correspondence dominates by almost twofold.

After loading packages and data as before (see script for plot 1), create a new column, "series_category," by extracting all characters before the comma (using the expression **,.***) from the original metadata column "Series," which also includes box and folder numbers (e.g., extracting "General Correspondence" from "General Correspondence, Box 004, Folder 001"):

```
data[, series_category := str_
remove(Series, ",.*")]
```

In the next step, create two lists of series categories, **series_personal** and **series_professional**, as defined in the finding aid (see the transforming data section of the script for plot 1).

Then follow by creating another column, "per_prof," and assigning to it either the name "Personal papers" or the name "Professional papers," depending on which of the two defined lists the document series category belongs to:

```
data[series_category %in% series_personal,
per_prof:="Personal papers"]
data[series_category %in% series_
professional, per_prof:="Professional
papers"]
```

In the next line, count documents for each of the two lists, personal versus professional, create a column to store the counting results, and then remove rows with missing values. The result of these operations is then assigned to the data table "per_prof_counts," as shown in table 3.2:

```
per_prof_counts <- na.omit(data[,
.(count=.N), by=per_prof])
```

The final step involves creating the bar plot by calling the **ggplot()** function.

Table 3.2
Plot 2 data: Bar plot comparing volumes of personal and professional papers

per_prof	count
Personal papers	12,052
Professional papers	6,146

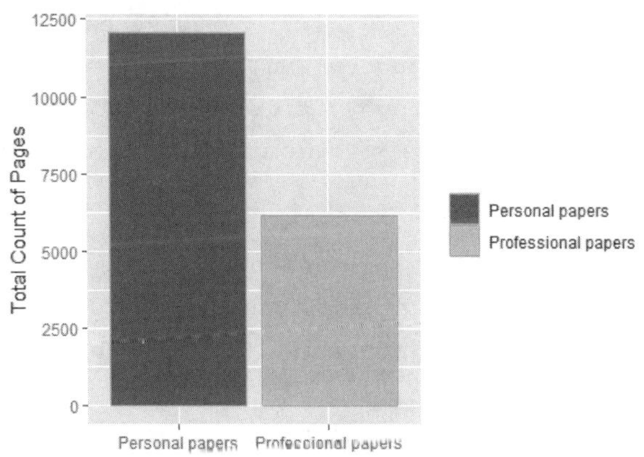

Figure 3.5
Plot 2—bar plot comparing volumes of personal and professional papers

R SCRIPT FOR PLOT 2

```
# plot_2
# loading packages
library(data.table)
library(ggplot2)
library(stringr)

# loading data
data <- fread("data/Tombaugh_Export_LTR.txt")

# transforming data
data[, series_category:=str_remove(Series, ",.*")]
series_personal <- c("General Correspondence",
                    "Family Correspondence",
                    "Fan Mail",
                    "Biographical Material",
                    "Educational Records",
                    "Subject Files",
                    "Planetary Observation",
                    "Telescopes and Optics",
                    "Organizations",
                    "Pluto Discovery Anniversary",
                    "Awards and Honors",
                    "Tombaugh Family",
                    "Unitarian Universalist Church",
                    "Writings")

series_professional <- c("Lowell Observatory",
                        "Arizona State Teachers College",
                        "UCLA",
                        "White Sands Proving Ground",
                        "New Mexico State University",
                        "NMSU Physical Science Lab",
                        "NMSU Research Files")
data[series_category %in% series_personal, per_prof:="Personal papers"]
data[series_category %in% series_professional, per_prof:="Professional papers"]
per_prof_counts <- na.omit(data[, .(count=.N), by=per_prof])

# plotting
ggplot(data=per_prof_counts,
       aes(x=per_prof, y=count, color = per_prof, fill = per_prof)) +
    scale_fill_manual(values=c("deeppink4", "cadetblue3")) +
    geom_col() +
    labs(x="", y="Total Count of Pages") +
    theme(axis.text.x = element_text(size=9, hjust=0.5),
          legend.title = element_blank())
```

```
# plotting
ggplot(data=per_prof_counts,
      aes(x=per_prof, y=count, color =
      per_prof, fill = per_prof)) +
   scale_fill_manual(values=c("deeppink4",
   "cadetblue3")) +
   geom_col() +
   labs(x="", y="Total Count of Pages") +
   theme(axis.text.x = element_
   text(size=9, hjust=0.5),
         legend.title = element_blank())
```

Use the newly created data table "per_prof _counts" as input data. Then define aesthetics, including the axes and the bar color and fill that indicates the category—personal or professional. The function **`scale_fill_manual()`** allows you to customize colors selected for the bars. In the next line, define the plot type. The **`geom_col()`** function creates the bar plot. This time no arguments are used. The **`labs()`** function defines the axis labels. In this plot, there is no label for the *x* axis. Instead, the category names appear below the bars. With function **`theme()`**, you define the font size (**`size = 9`**) and the centered location (**`hjust=0.5`**) of the tick labels ("Personal papers" and "Professional papers"). In the last line, by setting **`legend.title`** to **`element_blank()`**, you remove the title from the legend, which in this case would not add any information.

Question 3: How Many Documents in Each Category Were Created in Successive Years?

Plot 3 (figure 3.6) compares two time line graphs presented together. This chart provides insight into when personal and professional documents originated.

The comparison between the time lines shows that Tombaugh was exchanging personal letters pretty much his entire adult life. His professional correspondence time line reflects his engagements with five institutions. Evidently, his professional activities in the 1940s through the 1960s, when Tombaugh was working at Arizona State Teachers College, UCLA, the White Sands Proving Ground, and New Mexico State University, are best represented in the collection to date. The peak in 1929–30 in the personal papers category corresponds to Tombaugh's first year at Lowell Observatory and the discovery of Pluto, whereas the peak in 1980, again in the personal papers category, corresponds to the fiftieth anniversary of this discovery. Both events are well documented in the digital collection.

An additional step in transforming data and getting them ready for plotting is creating annual counts of document pages by personal and professional categories, stored in the data table called "per_prof_counts_by_year." A fragment of this data table is shown in table 3.3.

Next, call the **`ggplot()`** function again. A new element in this section is the **`facet_wrap()`** function, which lays out two plots in one figure:

```
facet_wrap(~per_prof, ncol=1,
scales="fixed") +
```

The tilde before **`per_prof`** makes the plots split by the values in the column "per_prof" ("Personal

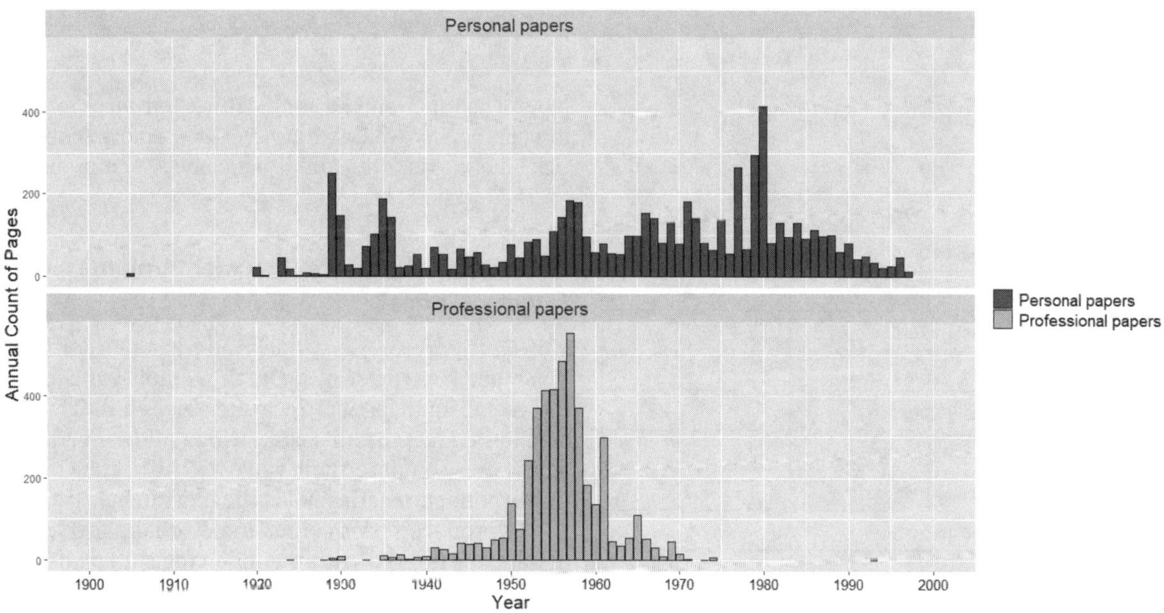

Figure 3.6
Plot 3—a comparison of two time line graphs for personal and professional papers

R SCRIPT FOR PLOT 3

Use the same initial steps as in the script for plots 1 and 2, namely loading packages and data as well as creating columns: "series_category," "per_prof," and "year" (see scripts for plots 1 and 2).

```
#plot_3
# transforming data continued
per_prof_counts_by_year <- na.omit(data[, .(count=.N),
                                        by=c("year", "per_prof")][order(year)])

# plotting
ggplot(data=per_prof_counts_by_year, aes(x=year,
                                         y=count,
                                         color = per_prof,
                                         fill = per_prof)) +
    scale_fill_manual(values=c("deeppink4", "cadetblue3")) +
    geom_col(color = "black") +
    scale_x_continuous(breaks = seq(1900, 2000, by = 10),
                       limits = c(1900, 2000)) +
    labs(x="Year", y="Annual Count of Pages") +
    facet_wrap(~per_prof, ncol=1, scales="fixed") +
    theme(strip.text.x = element_text(size = 16),
          axis.text.x = element_text(size = 12, colour = "black"),
          axis.title.x = element_text(size = 16, colour = "black"),
          axis.title.y = element_text(size = 16, colour = "black"),
          legend.text = element_text(size = 14, colour = "black"),
          legend.title = element_blank())
```

Table 3.3
Plot 3 data

year	per_prof	count
1905	Personal papers	7
1920	Personal papers	22
1921	Personal papers	1
1923	Personal papers	44
1924	Personal papers	17
1924	Professional papers	1
1925	Personal papers	1
1926	Personal papers	9

papers" and "Professional papers"). The parameter **`ncol=1`** lays out the plots in one column. The parameter **`scales="fixed"`** sets the same axis scale for both plots. The function **`theme()`** defines font sizes for titles in subplots, as well as font sizes and colors for axis *x* tick labels, axis titles, and legend labels. Again, the title for the legend is removed.

Question 4: What Are Document Volumes in Selected Series?

Plot 4a (figure 3.7) is a horizontal bar plot with volumes per specific series. On this graph we zoom in to see personal papers in a greater detail. The plot displays counts for all series, which allows readers to assess and compare their values. Visibly, the General Correspondence series holds the most items.

To produce series counts in personal papers, rows in data are filtered with the following statement:

```
series_category %in% series_personal
```

Extract only those rows for which the series cate-

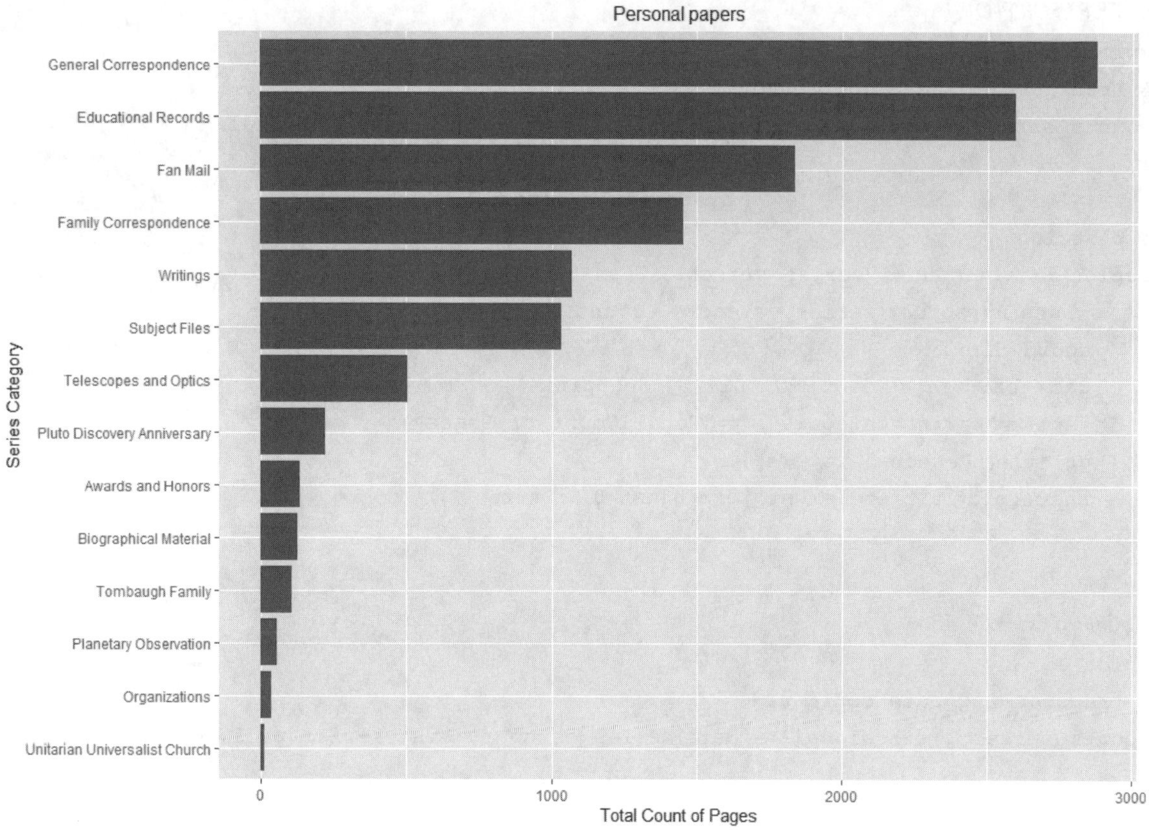

Figure 3.7
Plot 4a—horizontal bar plot showing volumes per specific series in personal papers

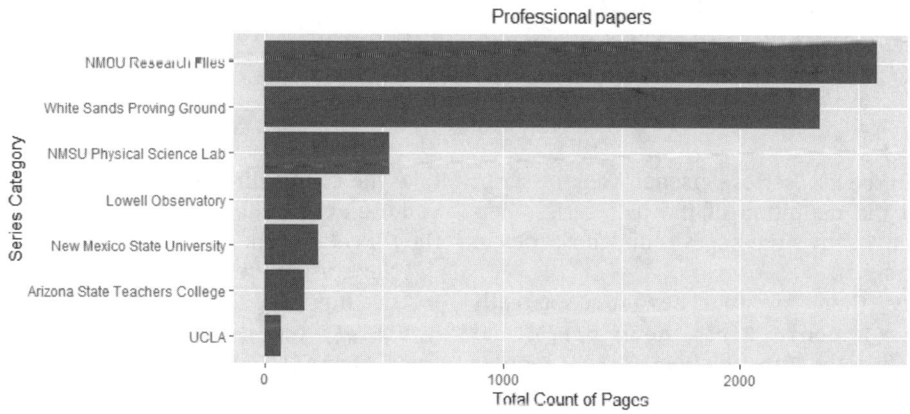

Figure 3.8
Plot 4b—horizontal bar plot showing volumes per specific series in professional papers

R SCRIPT FOR PLOT 4A

```
#plot_4a
# transforming data continued
counts_series_personal <- data[series_category %in% series_personal,
                              .(count=.N),
                              by=series_category]
# plotting
ggplot(data = counts_series_personal,
       aes(x=reorder(series_category, count), y=count)) +
    coord_flip() +
    geom_bar(stat='identity', fill = "deeppink4") +
    labs(x="Series Category", y="Total Count of Pages") +
    ggtitle("Personal papers") +
    theme(plot.title=element_text(hjust=0.5, size=12))
```

R SCRIPT FOR PLOT 4B

```
#plot_4b
# transforming data continued
counts_series_professional <- data[series_category %in% series_professional,
                                  .(count=.N),
                                  by=series_category]
# plotting
ggplot(data = counts_series_professional,
       aes(x=reorder(series_category, count), y=count)) +
    coord_flip() +
    geom_bar(stat='identity', fill = "deeppink4") +
    labs(y="Total Count of Pages", x="Series Category") +
    ggtitle("Professional papers") +
    theme(plot.title=element_text(hjust=0.5, size=12))
```

gory value is in the list "series_personal" (see the script for plot 2 for the definition of the list "series_ personal"). Table 3.4 shows the pages counts for series in personal papers.

In plotting, there are four new function calls here: **reorder()**, **coord_flip()**, **geom_bar()**, and **ggtitle()**. With the function **reorder()**, reorder the category levels by their counts. The **coord_flip()** function swaps *x* and *y* axes. Axis *y* maps the category count, and axis *x* maps category levels for column "series_category." Then, the call to the function **geom_bar()** with **stat='identity'** ensures that the heights of the bars correspond to the series counts. In general, the parameter **stat** defines the function on aggregated data (by default, **'count'**). You counted the records previously, so you want **geom_bar()** to take the counts directly, without aggregation. Hence, you use **stat='identity'**. The argument **fill** defines the fill color of the horizontal bars.

Next, using the function **labs()**, define the labels for the flipped *x* and *y* axes, and with the function **ggtitle()**, the title of the entire plot. The last function, **theme()**, helps defining the center position (**hjust=0.5**) and font size of the plot's title.

Plot 4b (figure 3.8) is another horizontal bar plot with volumes per series. It shows the distribution of series counts for professional papers. Here, the NMSU Research Files series holds the most records to date.

The same R code functions apply here. The only difference from plot 4a is that now we take into account only the column "series_professional" as displayed in table 3.5.

Table 3.4
Plot 4a data

series_category	count
General Correspondence	2,876
Fan Mail	1,839
Pluto Discovery Anniversary	220
Family Correspondence	1,451
Tombaugh Family	106
Planetary Observation	55
Telescopes and Optics	506
Awards and Honors	135
Biographical Material	124
Educational Records	2,595
Writings	1,067
Subject Files	1,030
Unitarian Universalist Church	12
Organizations	36

Table 3.5
Plot 4b data

series_category	count
Lowell Observatory	241
Arizona State Teachers College	168
UCLA	68
White Sands Proving Ground	2,340
New Mexico State University	226
NMSU Research Files	2,578
NMSU Physical Science Lab	525

Table 3.6
Plot 5a data

year	series_category	count
1905	General Correspondence	2
1928	General Correspondence	2
1927	General Correspondence	1
1925	General Correspondence	1
1933	Fan Mail	2
	Fan Mail	488
1957	Fan Mail	49
1958	Fan Mail	24
1959	Fan Mail	36
1956	Fan Mail	30

Question 5: When Were the Documents in Each Series Created? Is There Any Time Overlap?

Plot 5a (figure 3.9) is an aggregation of several time lines for selected series for comparison.

On these graphs, we can see the distributions of series in personal papers over the years. Again, we see corresponding peaks around 1980 in the Awards and Honors series and the Pluto Discovery Anniversary series. It was the fiftieth anniversary of the Pluto discovery event, "the Golden Year of the Ninth Planet", that brought so much recognition to Tombaugh.

Interestingly, Fan Mail's peak seems to correspond to the same event. Presently only the first few years of fan mail are included in our digital collection. But based on what we can see here, it looks like Tombaugh was not popular immediately after making his discovery. It was more toward the 1950s when his publicity really grew. The Planetary Observation series represents his early interests in astronomy, while the Telescopes and Optics series shows his lifelong engagement in constructing reflecting telescopes.

Here repeat the first steps from the previous plots, starting with plot 2. In the transforming data section, select a subset of series to include in the plot and assign the list to "series_personal." Then calculate annual counts for all series and title the resulting data table "annual_counts_series."

Using the function **`ggplot()`**, create multiple time lines in one plot. First, assign the data table "annual_count_series" to data with its rows filtered (with "series_category" values belonging to the "series_personal" list). A fragment of the "annual_counts_series" data table is shown in table 3.6.

In the next step, map the *x* axis to "year" and *y* axis to "count" in the aesthetics function (**`aes()`**). Then call the function **`geom_col()`** to create bar charts and choose the fill color for bars. With the function **`xlim()`**, define the range of years on the *x* axis. Next, define the plot title (with the function **`ggtitle()`**) and set its position to centered with the function **`theme()`** (horizontal adjustment, **`hjust=0.5`**). In the line, define axis labels with the function **`labs()`**.

Finally, call the **`facet_wrap()`** function, which arranges multiple plots (one for each level of "series_category") in three columns (**`ncol=3`**). Also, the *y* axis scaling is adjusted for each plot (**`scales = "free_y"`**), while x axis scaling stays the same. This is done to accommodate the different numbers of records in each series.

Plot 5b (figure 3.10) shows multiple time lines for professional papers for comparison.

Among several institutions that Tombaugh worked for, the correspondence associated with the Lowell Observatory, the White Sands Proving Ground, and New Mexico State University, including NMSU Physical Science Lab, are well represented in the digital

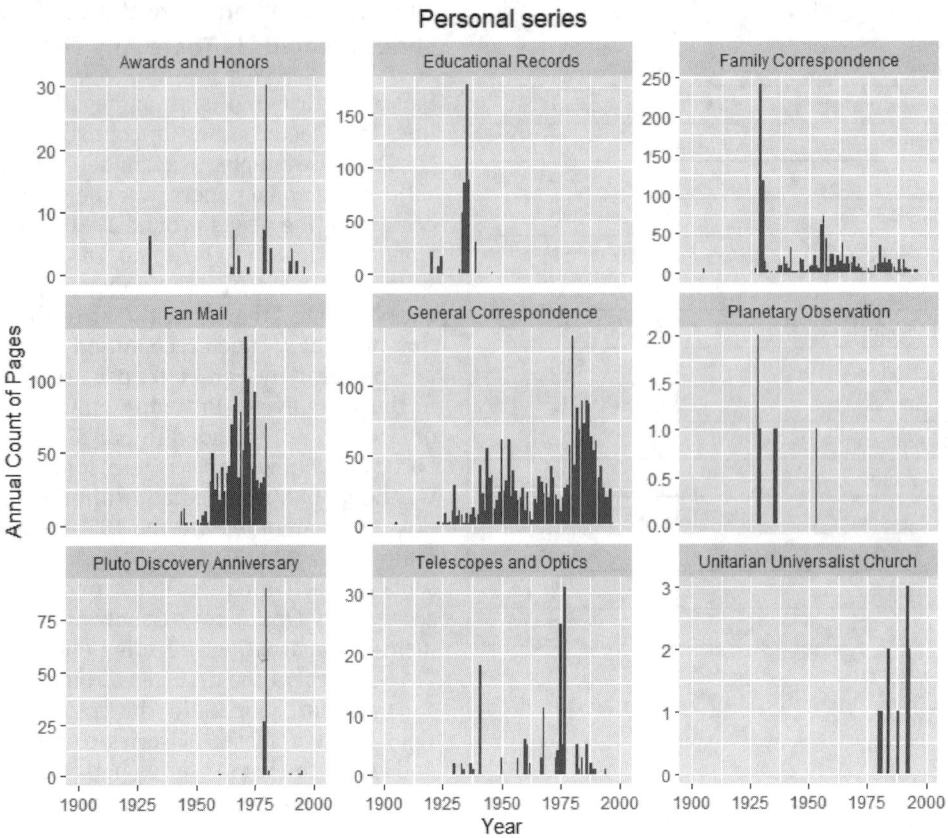

Figure 3.9
Plot 5a—set of time lines for selected series in personal papers

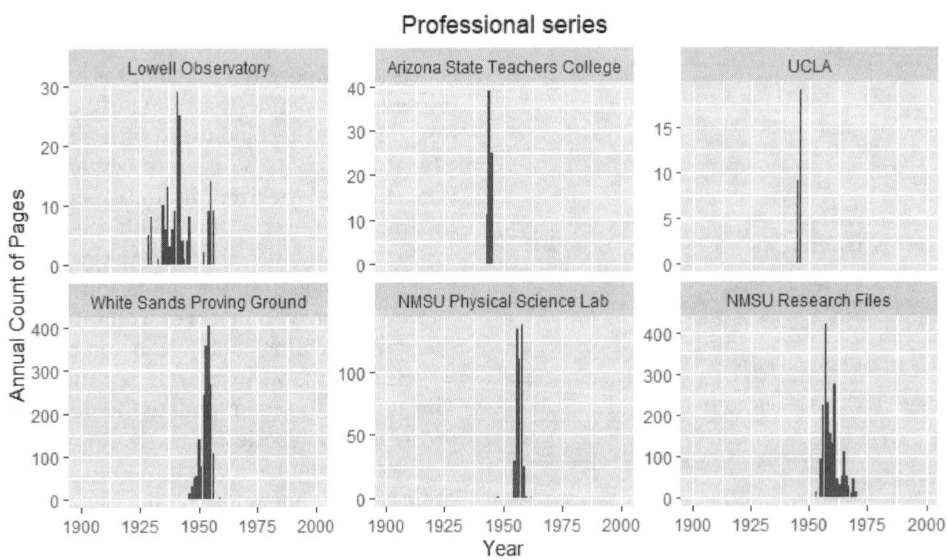

Figure 3.10
Plot 5b—set of time lines for selected series in professional papers

collection. Papers produced at the Arizona State Teachers College and UCLA are of more limited scope.

The same script is used here, only with a different subset of data and custom ordering of series categories.

After creating annual counts for all series ("annual_counts_series"), filter them down to "series_professional" and assign the name "annual_counts_professional" to the resulting data table. With the function **factor()**, order the levels of the "series_category" column in "annual_counts_professional" as defined in the list assigned to parameter **levels**:

```
levels = c("Lowell Observatory",
           "Arizona State Teachers
           College",
           "UCLA",
           "White Sands Proving Ground",
           "NMSU Physical Science Lab",
           "NMSU Research Files"))
```

Table 3.7
Plot 5b data

year	series_category	count
1955	Lowell Observatory	14
1956	Lowell Observatory	9
1943	Arizona State Teachers College	11
1945	Arizona State Teachers College	25
	Arizona State Teachers College	93
1944	Arizona State Teachers College	39
1945	UCLA	9
1946	UCLA	19
	UCLA	40
1954	White Sands Proving Ground	404
	White Sands Proving Ground	594
1953	White Sands Proving Ground	359

R SCRIPT FOR PLOT 5A

```
#plot_5a
# transforming data continued
series_personal <- c("General Correspondence",
                     "Family Correspondence",
                     "Fan Mail",
                     "Educational Records",
                     "Planetary Observation",
                     "Telescopes and Optics",
                     "Pluto Discovery Anniversary",
                     "Awards and Honors",
                     "Unitarian Universalist Church")
annual_counts_series <- data[, .(count=.N),
                             by=c("year",
                                  "series_category")]
# plotting
ggplot(data=annual_counts_series[series_category %in% series_personal,],
       aes(x=year,
           y=count)) +
    geom_col(fill = "deeppink4") +
    xlim(1900, 2000) +
    ggtitle("Personal series") +
    theme(plot.title=element_text(hjust=0.5)) +
    labs(x="Year",
         y="Annual Count of Pages") +
    facet_wrap(~series_category, ncol=3, scales = "free_y")
```

In the next step, implement reordering of "annual_counts_professional" by assigning the newly defined "ordered_factor" to the column "series_category." Table 3.7 shows a fragment of the data set for plot 5b.

Finally, subject "annual_counts_professional" to the **ggplot()** function with the same parameters as in the plot 5a, keeping the same color (**"deeppink4"**) and changing just the title (**"Professional series"**).

Question 6: Who among Tombaugh's Correspondents Was Most Prolific as Represented in the Collection?

Plot 6 (figure 3.11) is a horizontal bar chart with flipped coordinates. It compares volumes of letters written by different authors. It shows total counts of records per selected creator. As expected, Tombaugh,

R SCRIPT FOR PLOT 5B

```
#plot_5b
# transforming data continued
annual_counts_series <- data[, .(count=.N),
                             by=c("year",
                             "series_category")]

series_professional <- c("Lowell Observatory",
                         "Arizona State Teachers College",
                         "UCLA",
                         "White Sands Proving Ground",
                         "NMSU Physical Science Lab",
                         "NMSU Research Files")

annual_counts_professional <-
       annual_counts_series[series_category %in% series_professional,]

ordered_factor = factor(annual_counts_professional[, series_category],
                        levels = c("Lowell Observatory",
                                   "Arizona State Teachers College",
                                   "UCLA",
                                   "White Sands Proving Ground",
                                   "NMSU Physical Science Lab",
                                   "NMSU Research Files"))

annual_counts_professional[, series_category:=ordered_factor]

# plotting
ggplot(data=annual_counts_professional,
       aes(x=year,
           y=count)) +
     geom_col(fill = "deeppink4") +
     xlim(1900, 2000) +
     ggtitle("Professional series") +
     theme(plot.title=element_text(hjust=0.5)) +
     labs(x="Year",
          y="Annual Count of Pages") +
     facet_wrap(~series_category, ncol=3, scales = "free_y")
```

the author of a massive number of letters, is totally off the chart. Hence, there is no bar representing him at the top of the plot. If his correspondence were included, differences among other creators would not be well represented on the plot. Interestingly, based on the evidence in figure 3.11, Tombaugh corresponded most intensely with his students Brad Smith, Charles Capen, and Jimmy Robinson. His exchanges with his family members and colleagues come right after.

This chart also shows a problem with inconsistent format for the creators' names. Brad Smith is listed here twice, as "Smith, Brad, 1931-" and "Smith, Brad, 1931-2018." Apparently, records added more recently include an authority name updated after Smith's death. Evidently, such inconsistency influences the outcome to a considerable extent. Visualizations provide a remarkable insight into quality of metadata and allow for quick identification of issues.

After loading needed packages and data, extract the column "Creator" from the original data as a list of strings and assign it to the column "creator_column":

```
creator_column <- data[, Creator]
```

Unfortunately, some entries in the column "Creator" contain groups of creators (separated by semicolons), as shown in the example in table 3.8.

In order to calculate counts of pages for each creator correctly, first collect a long list of individual names of creators by splitting multiple names where needed, and then count occurrences of individual names. Collection of individual names is done in a **for** loop. First, create an empty list for individual names, "creator_list." Next, set the loop to traverse all entries in the column "creator_column":

```
for(column_entry in creator_column)
```

Table 3.8
Plot 6 raw data

Creator
Alyn, Scott; Adams, John; Adel, Arthur, 1908-1994; Solecki, Thomas J.
Robinson, Michael

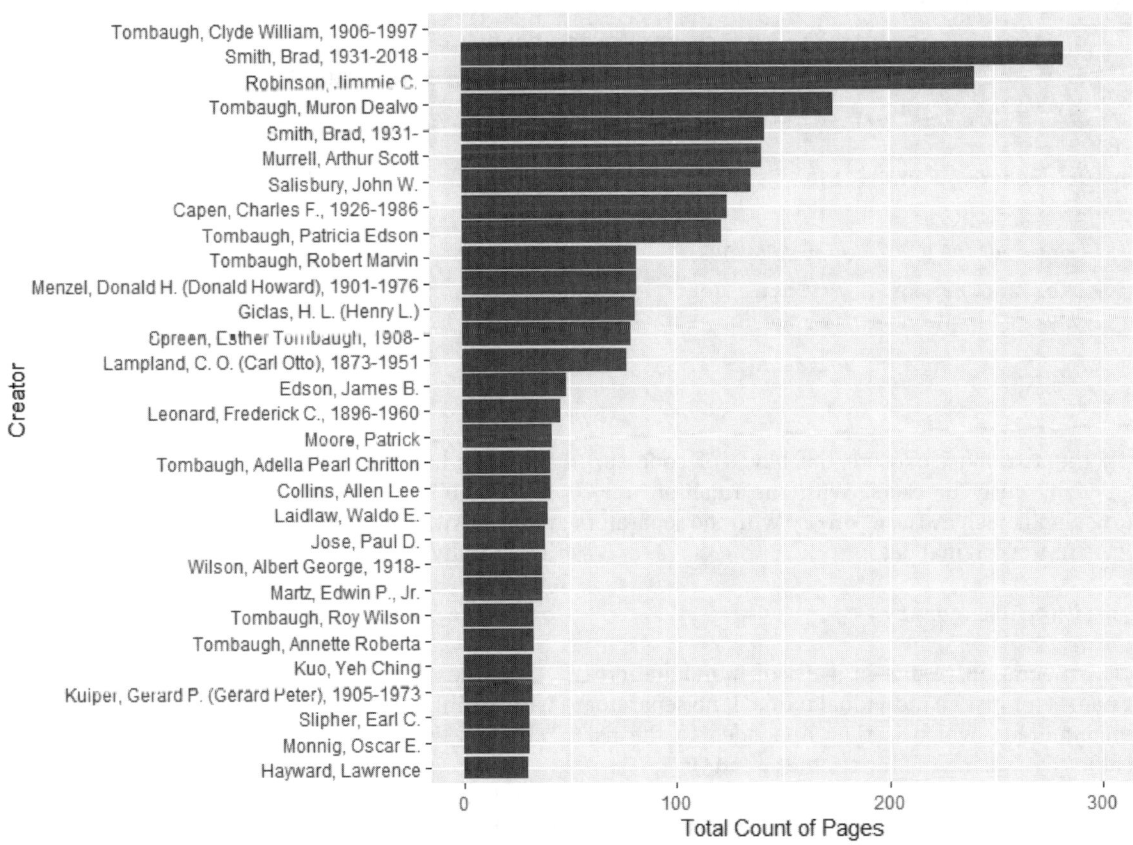

Figure 3.11
Plot 6—horizontal bar comparing volumes of documents by creators

R SCRIPT FOR PLOT 6

```
# plot_6
# loading packages
library(data.table)
library(ggplot2)
library(stringr)

# loading data
data <- fread("data/Tombaugh_Export_LTR.txt")

# transforming data
creator_column <- data[, Creator]

creators_list <- list()
for(column_entry in creator_column) {
   creators_list <- append(creators_list, strsplit(column_entry, "; "))
}
creators_list <- unlist(creators_list)

creators <- data.table(Creator = creators_list)
creators[, Creator:=str_remove(Creator, ";"), ]

creator_counts <-
    creators[, .(count=.N), by=Creator][order(count,
                                               decreasing = TRUE)]

# plotting
ggplot(creator_counts[1:30, ], aes(x=reorder(Creator, count), y=count)) +
    coord_flip() +
    geom_col(fill = "deeppink4") +
    labs(x="Creator", y="Total Count of Pages") +
    ylim(0, 300)
```

In the **for** loop, execute the block of code surrounded by curly brackets. With the function **strsplit()**, split each **column_entry** with the separator **"; "** as in the original data:

```
strsplit(column_entry, "; ")
```

This operation results in a list of individual creator names (or just an individual name, if no separator is encountered), which is then appended to the list "creators_list," using the function **append()**:

```
append(creators_list, strsplit(column_
entry, "; "))
```

The new list is assigned back to the list "creators_list." After the loop ends, "creators_list" contains both individual names and, occasionally, lists of names. With the function **unlist()**, it is turned into a list of individual names:

```
creators_list <- unlist(creators_list)
```

In the next step, create the data table "creators," with a single column "Creator," holding elements of "creators_list":

```
creators <- data.table(Creator =
creators_list)
```

Then, from the newly made "creators," produce counts of pages by "Creator" in descending order and

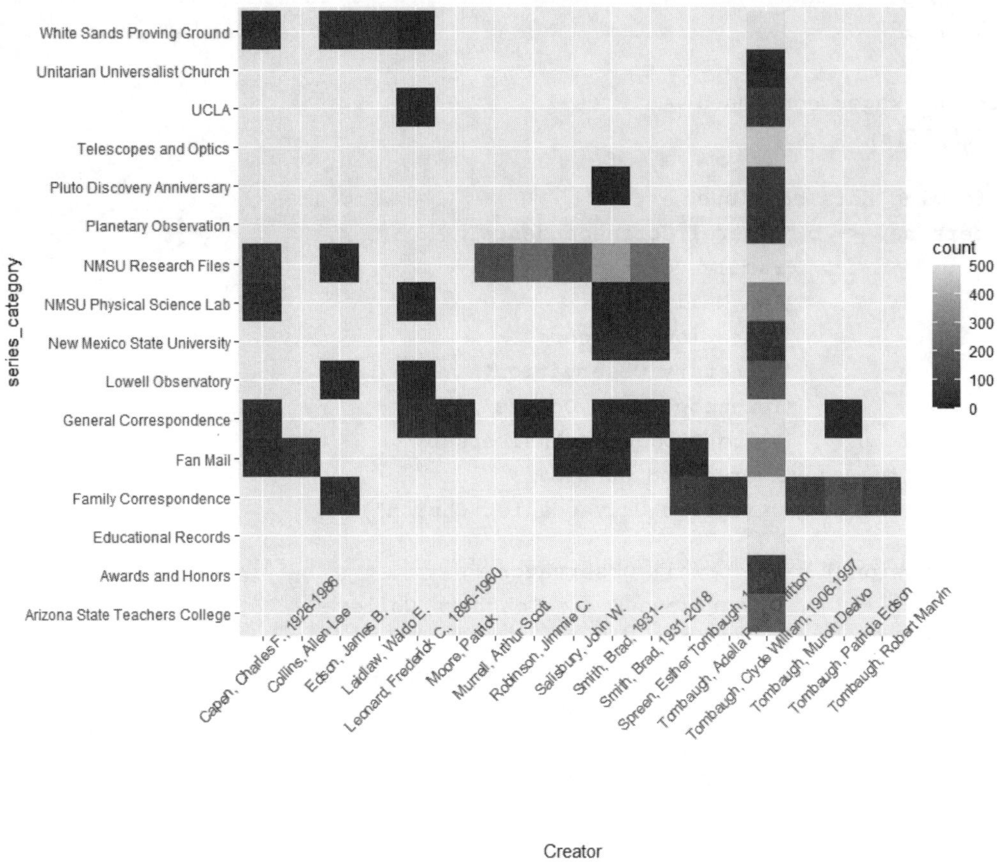

Figure 3.12
Plot 7—heat map showing the distribution of documents across series for selected creators

store them in the data table "creator_counts" (fragment shown in table 3.9).

At this point, feed the first thirty rows of "creator_counts" (`creator_counts[1:30, ]`) as **data** to the `ggplot()` function. In the aesthetics function (`aes()`), axis *x* maps creator names (column "Creator") ordered by "count," and axis *y* maps "count." Next, the *x* and *y* axes are swapped using the function `coord_flip()`, and a bar chart is created with the function `geom_col()`, colored in `"deepink4"`. Finally, *x* and *y* axis labels are created with the function `labs()`, and a range for axis *y* is set with the `ylim()` function.

Question 7: What Is the Distribution of Document Counts across Series for Individual Creators?

Plot 7 (figure 3.12) is a heat map. Heat maps show a color-coded view of multidimensional data. Here we look at three variables—creators, series, and counts—to see patterns of count distributions across series and creators. Missing values are not colored. This heat map provides a great way to identify who contributed to what correspondence series or, to put it differently, in what series one should look to find letters of a particular author. Apparently, some authors appear in different series, which may mean that they worked with Tombaugh on more than one project.

Table 3.9
Plot 6 data

Creator	count
Tombaugh, Clyde William, 1906-1997	10,484
Smith, Brad, 1931-2018	282
Robinson, Jimmie C.	241
Tombaugh, Muron Dealvo	174
Smith, Brad, 1931-	142
Murrell, Arthur Scott	141
Salisbury, John W.	136
Capen, Charles F., 1926-1986	125
Tombaugh, Patricia Edson	122

R SCRIPT FOR PLOT 7

```
# plot_7
# loading packages continued
library(viridis)

# transforming data continued
series_personal <- c("General Correspondence",
                     "Family Correspondence",
                     "Fan Mail",
                     "Educational Records",
                     "Planetary Observation",
                     "Telescopes and Optics",
                     "Pluto Discovery Anniversary",
                     "Awards and Honors",
                     "Unitarian Universalist Church")

series_professional <- c("Lowell Observatory",
                         "Arizona State Teachers College",
                         "UCLA",
                         "White Sands Proving Ground",
                         "New Mexico State University",
                         "NMSU Physical Science Lab",
                         "NMSU Research Files")

data[, series_category:=str_remove(Series, ",.*")]

data <- data[series_category %in% series_personal |
                    series_category %in% series_professional, ]

counts_creators_series = data[Creator %like% creator_counts[1, Creator],
                              .(count=.N),
                              by=series_category]
counts_creators_series[, Creator:=creator_counts[1, Creator]]

for(creator_name in creator_counts[2:20, Creator]) {
    counts_t = data[Creator %like% creator_name,
                    .(count=.N),
                    by=series_category]
    counts_t[, Creator:=creator_name]
    counts_creators_series <- rbind(counts_creators_series,
                                    counts_t)
}

# plotting
ggplot(data=counts_creators_series,
       aes(x=Creator,
           y=series_category,
           fill=count)) +
    geom_tile() +
    scale_fill_viridis(limits = c(0, 500), oob = scales::squish) +
    theme(axis.text.x = element_text(angle = 45))
```

Table 3.10
Plot 7 data

series_category	count	Creator
Awards and Honors	52	Tombaugh, Clyde William, 1906-1997
Educational Records	2,556	Tombaugh, Clyde William, 1906-1997
White Sands Proving Ground	1,616	Tombaugh, Clyde William, 1906-1997
Unitarian Universalist Church	4	Tombaugh, Clyde William, 1906-1997
New Mexico State University	45	Tombaugh, Clyde William, 1906-1997
NMSU Research Files	1,163	Tombaugh, Clyde William, 1906-1997
NMSU Physical Science Lab	285	Tombaugh, Clyde William, 1906-1997
General Correspondence	1	Smith, Brad, 1931-2018
NMSU Research Files	243	Smith, Brad, 1931-2018
NMSU Physical Science Lab	3	Smith, Brad, 1931-2018
New Mexico State University	23	Smith, Brad, 1931-2018
General Correspondence	2	Robinson, Jimmie C.
NMSU Research Files	239	Robinson, Jimmie C.
Family Correspondence	66	Tombaugh, Muron Dealvo

As before, start with loading needed packages and data. To create a heat map we need an additional package, called viridis, with color scales. This package needs to be installed before loading it.

Here, the data table "creator_counts," created for plot 6, is used. As in the former plots, define "series_personal" and "series_professional" lists of "series_categories." Next, create a new column, "series_category," by extracting all characters before the comma from the original metadata column "Series," which also included box and folder numbers (e.g., "General Correspondence" from "General Correspondence, Box 004, Folder 001"):

```
data[, series_category := str_
remove(Series, ",.*")]
```

Now, filter the rows of data down to series category values that are in either of the lists, personal or professional. Then, create the first segment of "counts_creators_series" containing counts of just Clyde Tombaugh's papers per series category. For this purpose, filter rows down to those that contain the creator's name. (We may encounter a group of creators' names, not just an individual one.)

```
data[Creator %like% creator_counts[1,
Creator],
```

Then add an extra column, "Creator," with the creator's name. With the largest number of documents, Tombaugh is in the first position in the data table "creator_counts":

```
counts_creators_series = data[Creator
%like% creator_counts[1, Creator],
            .(count=.N),
            by=series_category]
counts_creators_series[, Creator:=creator_
counts[1, Creator]]
```

Do the same with the selected creators in the **`for`** loop, where we concatenate vertically "counts_creators_series" with data segments corresponding to subsequent creators. A fragment of "counts_creator_series" is shown in table 3.10.

In the plotting section, define the heat map using the **`geom_tile()`** function with **`data`** as **`counts_creators_series`** and **`Creator`** and **`series_category`** as *x* and *y* axes, colored according to **`count`** values. Then define the color scale using the function **`scale_fill_viridis()`** with range of count values between 0 and 500 (**`limits = c(0, 500)`**), with truncating values outside of the range (**`oob = scales::squish`**). Finally, using the function **`theme()`**, define the angle of the *x* axis tick labels as 45 degrees.

Question 8: What Are the Most Dominant Terms in a Given Correspondence Series?

Plot 8a (figure 3.13) is a word cloud. A word cloud, known also as a tag cloud or a term cloud, is a visual representation of text data. This type of visualization is suitable for quickly perceiving the most frequent terms and, perhaps, getting at the essence of the text. The prominence of the relative count of each term is shown with font size or color.

R SCRIPT FOR PLOT 8A

```
# plot_8a
# loading packages
library(data.table)
library(stringr)
library(NLP)
library(tm)
library(corpus)
library(wordcloud2)

# loading data
data <- fread("data/Tombaugh_Export_LTR.txt")

# transforming data
data[, series_category:=str_remove(Series, ",.*")]

txt_column <- "OCR"
txt_column = noquote(txt_column)

data[[txt_column]] <- as.character(data[[txt_column]])
data[[txt_column]] <- tolower(data[[txt_column]])
data[[txt_column]] <- tm::removeNumbers(data[[txt_column]])
data[[txt_column]] <- str_squish(data[[txt_column]])
data[[txt_column]] <- str_replace_all(data[[txt_column]], "[^[:alnum:]]", " ")

data_subset <- data[series_category=="Pluto Discovery Anniversary", ]

corpus <- Corpus(VectorSource(data_subset[, OCR]))
corpus <- tm_map(corpus, stripWhitespace)
corpus <- tm_map(corpus, removeWords, stopwords("english"))

dtm <- TermDocumentMatrix(corpus)
m <- as.matrix(dtm)
v <- sort(rowSums(m), decreasing=TRUE)
d <- data.table(word = names(v), freq=v)

# add selected bigrams
d_t1 <- data.table(word="las cruces",
                   freq=sum(data_subset[, str_count(OCR, "las cruces")]))
d_t2 <- data.table(word="white sands",
                   freq=sum(data_subset[, str_count(OCR, "white sands")]))
d_t3 <- data.table(word="new mexico",
                   freq=sum(data_subset[, str_count(OCR, "new mexico")]))

d <- rbind(d, d_t1, d_t2, d_t3)[order(freq, decreasing = TRUE)]

# plotting
wordcloud2(d[1:150,], shape="triangle-forward")
```

The terms in this cloud were extracted from the Pluto Discovery Anniversary series in personal papers. As can be seen, the terms displayed in figure 3.13 correspond to the occasion. The word cloud in figure 3.14, representing a different series, displays clear difference in vocabulary used.

Plot 8b (figure 3.14) is a word cloud for the Arizona State Teachers College series. Plainly, Tombaugh taught navigation there.

In order to build a word cloud, first load the needed packages and data. Next, create a new column, "series_category," as in the former plots, by extracting from values in the column "Series" strings of characters occurring up to the first comma.

Then select the column with OCR and preprocess it. The preprocessing of the "OCR" column involves turning its content in place into text format (with the function **`as.character()`**) in lower case (with the function **`tolower()`**) and removing all digits (with the function **`tm::removeNumbers()`**). Next, turn all non-alphanumeric characters into white space. For this operation, use the function **`str_replace_all()`** with a regular expression pattern **`"[^[:alnum:]]"`**. Then, remove excess white spaces with the function **`str_squish()`**.

After preprocessing, select rows for a given series of interest (in **`data_subset`**) and turn them into a corpus (i.e., a set of text documents) by applying to the column "OCR" a sequence of functions, **`VectorSource()`** and **`Corpus()`**. The function **`VectorSource()`** produces a vector of text documents, each corresponding to a row in OCR column. Then, the function **`Corpus()`** turns the resulting vector of documents into a corpus of documents.

Next, use three function calls to remove English stop words from the corpus. The function **`tm_map()`** calls the function **`removeWords()`**, which deletes from the corpus the English stop words returned as a list by **`stopwords("english")`**.

Then turn the corpus with all documents into a term-document matrix ("term_doc_matrix_tdm") with terms in rows and documents (or records) in columns. Each entry in this matrix is the count of a given term in a given record. In the next step, turn the term-document matrix into an R matrix ("term_doc_matrix"), shown in table 3.11.

Some words displayed in the matrix may not make much sense because OCR may not be capable of rendering handwritten texts.

In the next step, sort the term-document R matrix by word counts across all records. The sorting outcome (a vector, "word_frequencies_vector") is cast as a data table "word_frequencies" that has two columns, "word" and "freq," shown in table 3.12.

We may want to add bigrams, such as "las cruces," "white sands," or "new mexico," to the table "word_frequencies," For each bigram, create a single-row data table with two columns, "word" and "freq." Then assign the bigram to column "word" and its frequency to column "freq." The frequency of the bigram is calculated as a sum of counts of its occurrences across all rows of the table "data_subset," for example:

```
freq=sum(data_subset[, str_count(OCR, "las
cruces")])
```

Using the function **`rbind()`**, append vertically all the bigram data tables to the table "word_frequencies" and sort it with the function **`order()`** into descending order by frequency.

After that, call the function **`wordcloud2()`** with two arguments: the data table "word_frequencies" limited to the top 150 entries, and **`shape`**. Different shapes for the cloud, including triangles, circles, pentagons, and diamonds, can be selected.

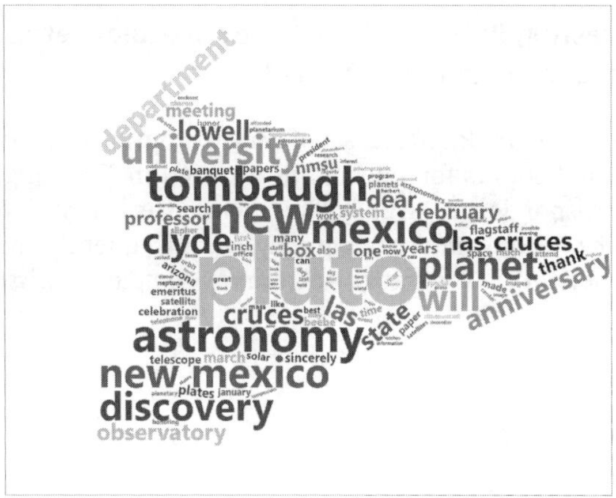

Figure 3.13
Plot 8a—word cloud for the Pluto Discovery Anniversary series

Figure 3.14
Plot 8b—word cloud for the Arizona State Teachers College series

Question 9: How Often Were Particular Terms Used in Subsequent Years?

Plot 9 (figure 3.15) is a set of time histograms showing annual counts for selected terms used in Tombaugh's correspondence over years. While terms such as *home*, *money*, and *photography* were frequently mentioned over Tombaugh's lifetime, *computer*, *missile*, and *satellites* are more time-bound.

As before, load the packages and data, use the function **setnames()** to change the column name, and then use the function **setcolorder()** to place the column "date_original" at the leftmost position in the table for easier examining of the table. Then create a new column, "year," by extracting four-digit year values from dates with the use of the function **str_extract()** and

R SCRIPT FOR PLOT 9

```
# plot_9
# loading packages
library(data.table)
library(ggplot2)
library(stringr)

# loading data
data <- fread("data/Tombaugh_Export_LTR.txt")

# transforming data
setnames(data, "Date Original", "date_original")
setcolorder(data, "date_original")
data[, year := as.numeric(str_extract(date_original, "\\d{4}"))]

selected_terms <- c("photography",
                    "home",
                    "money",
                    "satellites",
                    "missile",
                    "computer")
term_count_year <- data.table(year=numeric(),
                              annual_count=numeric(),
                              term=character())
for(i in c(1:length(selected_terms))) {
    term_count <- data[, .(year,
                          count=str_count(OCR, selected_terms[i]))]
    term_count_year_t <- term_count[, .(annual_count=sum(count)),
                                    by=year][order(year)]
    term_count_year_t[, term:=selected_terms[i]]
    term_count_year <- rbind(term_count_year,
                             term_count_year_t)
}

# plotting
ggplot(data=term_count_year, aes(x=year, annual_count)) +
   geom_col(fill="deeppink4") +
   facet_wrap(~term, ncol=3, scales = "free_y") +
   xlim(1900, 2000)
```

the regular expressions pattern (`"\\d{4}"`).

In the next step, select a list of terms for time line display. Then create an empty data table called "term_count_year" with columns "year," "annual count," and "term." This table will store annual counts of all selected terms.

In a **for** loop, for each of the selected terms, create a two-column data table, "term_count," with a column "count," with counts of a given term in each document, and a column "year." Based on this data table, calculate annual counts of the given term and store them in the data table "term_count_year_t." Add to it another column, "term," with the actual term. At this point, append the table "term_count_year_t" vertically to the table "term_count_year," which stores annual counts for all the selected terms. Table 3.13 shows how it looks for the term *photography.*

In the plotting section, use the function **ggplot()** with data table "term_count_year" as **data**. Using the function **aes()**, define axes *x* and *y*, as "year" and "annual count" respectively. Then call the function **geom_col()** to draw a plot and define color fill for bars (**"deeppink4"**). Another function, **facet_wrap()**, places six histograms together on one plot. Each histogram corresponds to one of the selected terms. The argument **~ term** splits data for each subplot according to values in the column "term." Another argument, **ncol**, defines the number of columns in the arrangement of subplots, and the next argument, **scales = "free_y"**, means that each subplot has its own optimal vertical scale. Finally, with the function **xlim()**, define the range of values for the *x* axis.

Question 10: Where Did Fan Letters Come From?

Plot 10a (figure 3.16) is an interactive map of Tombaugh's fans across the world. The dots represent locations from which Tombaugh received fan mail. Each dot corresponds to a letter. If a user hovers over or clicks on a dot, the corresponding address is displayed in a pop-up window. The digital collection holds just a representative sample of fan mail received by Tombaugh over the years.

Plot 10b (figure 3.17) is another interactive map, this time of the United States, showing locations of fan mail authors in a greater detail. Again, each dot represents a fan letter.

Before creating a script for the maps, set up an account with Google Maps to obtain the API key and get access to Google's services.[10] This step is necessary to produce geospatial coordinates (longitude and latitude) from addresses.

Start with loading packages and data. The data file has a column named "addresses" that holds all addresses extracted from the envelopes sent to Tombaugh. We use here only names of cities, states, and countries. We store the content of the file in the data table "fan_mail_locations." In the next step, using the function **register_google()**, register your R session with Google Maps Platform with the previously obtained API key. Next, transform the data. Specifically, create a list of addresses ("addresses_list") from the column "addresses" in the data table "fan_mail_locations." Then, call the function **geocode()** with **addresses_list** as **data** to get the coordinates for each address. Store the results in the data table

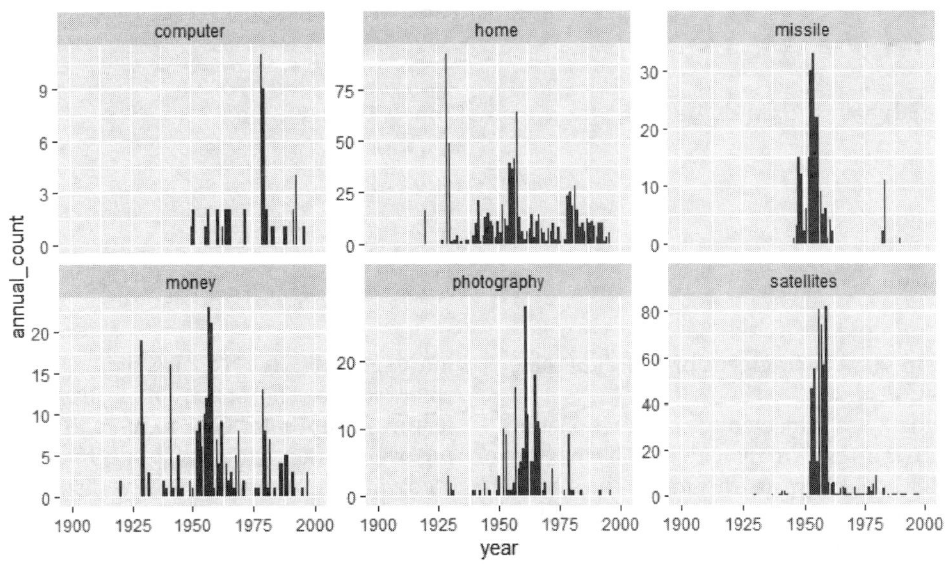

Figure 3.15
Plot 9—set of histograms for selected terms

R SCRIPT FOR PLOTS 10A AND 10B

```
# plot_10
# loading packages
library(data.table)
library(ggmap)
library(leaflet)

# loading data
fan_mail_locations <- fread("Fan_mail_addresses.csv")

# transforming data
register_google(key = "...")

addresses_list <- c(fan_mail_locations[, addresses])

geocode_addresses <- geocode(addresses_list,
                             output = "latlona",
                             source = "google")
geocode_addresses <- as.data.table(geocode_addresses)

# plotting
fan_map <- leaflet(data=geocode_addresses)
fan_map <- addTiles(fan_map)
fan_map <- addCircleMarkers(fan_map,
                            ~lon,
                            ~lat,
                            radius = 3,
                            color = 'DeepPink',
                            stroke = FALSE, fillOpacity = 0.8,
                            popup = ~as.character(address),
                            label = ~as.character(address))
print(fan_map)

geocode_addresses_usa <- geocode_addresses[lon >= -125 &
                                           lon <= -65 &
                                           lat >= 25 &
                                           lat <= 50, ]
```

"geocode_addresses." A fragment of this data table is shown in table 3.14.

Now the data are subjected to the function **leaflet()**, which creates a map widget. The next two function calls add layers to the map. The function **addTiles()** adds a tiled map. The function **addCircleMarkers()** adds circle markers to to "fan_map" at locations defined by the corresponding longitude and latitude values (coming from columns "lon" and "lat" in the data table "geocode_addresses"). The function **addCircleMarkers()** also defines markers' radius, color, stroke, and opacity as well as two interactive features (**popup** for clicking on and **label** for hovering over markers) to display specific addresses associated with the markers. Finally, display the map with the function **print()**.

To display the second map limited to the US (plot 10b), filter "geocode_addresses" to the ones in the specified range of longitudes and latitudes (see the last command in the script for plot 10) and then repeat

Table 3.11
Plot 8a data 1

	1	2	3	4	5	6	7	8	9	10
abstract	1	0	0	0	0	0	0	0	0	0
address	1	0	0	0	0	0	0	0	0	0
afternoon	1	0	0	0	0	0	0	0	0	0
also	1	0	0	0	0	0	1	0	0	0
anniversary	2	0	1	0	1	1	0	0	1	1
announce	1	0	0	0	0	0	0	0	0	0
associated	1	0	0	0	0	0	0	0	0	0
astronomers	1	0	0	0	0	0	0	0	0	0
astronomy	3	0	3	0	0	5	1	0	0	2
attend	1	0	1	0	0	0	0	0	0	0
banquet	1	0	1	0	0	0	0	0	0	0

Table 3.12
Plot 8a data 2

word	freq
pluto	298
new	181
astronomy	152
tombaugh	151
mexico	139
new mexico	136
planet	132
university	129
discovery	128

Table 3.13
Plot 9 data

year	annual_count	term
1945	0	photography
1946	1	photography
1947	0	photography
1948	0	photography
1949	1	photography
1950	3	photography
1951	0	photography
1952	10	photography
1953	9	photography

Table 3.14
Plot 10 data

lon	lat	address
-74.2037566	40.805378	glen ridge, nj 07028, usa
-103.7999509	40.2502582	fort morgan, co 80701, usa
29.3940979	30.8421333	el-hamam, el hamam, matrouh governorate, egypt
-69.9312117	18.4860575	santo domingo, dominican republic
-76.6147395	2.4448143	popayán, cauca, colombia
-77.042754	-12.0463731	lima, peru
144.9861397	-37.9159683	brighton beach, victoria, australia
-106.0691004	28.6329957	chihuahua, mexico
-61.5766664	-32.4751189	las rosas, santa fe province, argentina
-0.1277583	51.5073509	london, uk
-110.9747108	32.2226066	tucson, az, usa

Table 3.15
Plot 11 data

year	annual_count	type
2015	644	Created
2016	888	Created
2017	2,565	Created
2018	6,046	Created
2019	3,299	Created
2020	5,580	Created
2015	644	Modified
2016	887	Modified
2017	2,561	Modified
2018	6,039	Modified
2019	3,305	Modified
2020	5,586	Modified
2013	2	Digitized
2014	6	Digitized
2015	12,609	Digitized
2016	2,532	Digitized

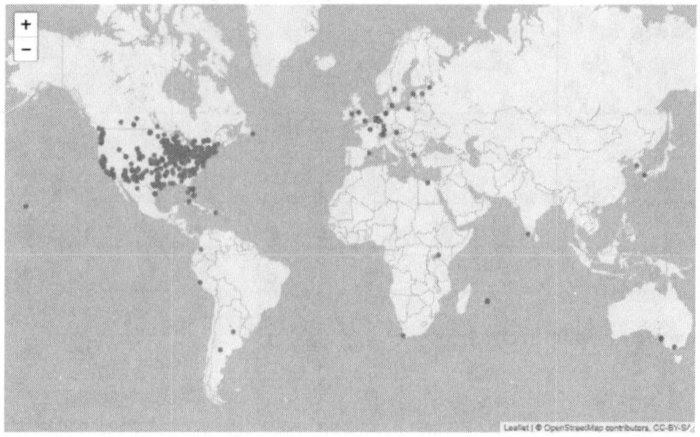

Figure 3.16
Plot 10a—interactive world map of Tombaugh's fans

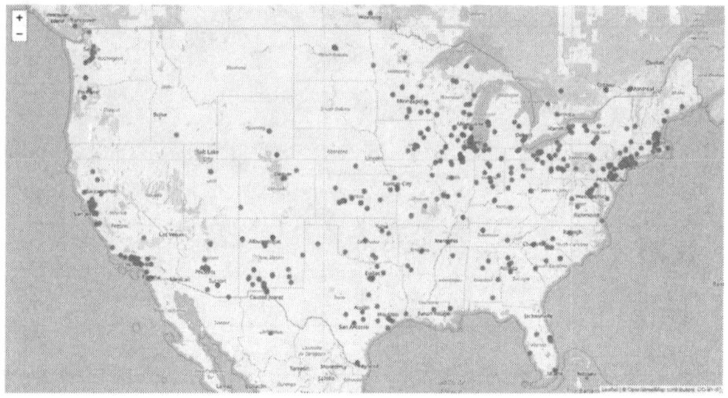

Figure 3.17
Plot 10b—interactive US map of Tombaugh's fans

Table 3.16
Plot 12 data

series_category	count
NMSU Research Center	107
Tombaugh Family	106
	97
Legal Size Files	90
Photographs	73
UCLA	68
Planetary Observation	55
Organizations	36
Miscellaneous	25
NMSU Research Files Box 115	24
Unitarian Universalist Church	12
NMSU Research Files Box	12
NMSU Research Files Box 116	8
NMSU Research Files Box 111	5
Gacharna	1

the sequence of commands with the filtered addresses ("geocode_addresses_usa"), starting with the call to function **`leaflet()`**.

Question 11: How Has the Collection Developed over Time?

Plot 11 (figure 3.18) is a set of three histograms stacked together. The histograms show annual counts of documents that were digitized, submitted to CONTENTdm (created), and modified, respectively. Based on the presented data, most of scanning work was done in 2015, whereas work on metadata and quality control intensified in 2018 and 2020.

To create this plot, we use three time-related columns, "Date digital," "Date created," and "Date modified," from the data table "data." "Date digital" refers to the date a document was scanned. "Date created" refers to the date a record was created, and "Date modified," to the last date when the record was changed.

As usual, first load packages and data. Then follow the usual set of procedures to produce annual counts of time events for each type: digital, created, and modified. To do so, use the function **`setnames()`** to change

R SCRIPT FOR PLOT 11

```
# plot_11
# loading packages
library(data.table)
library(ggplot2)
library(stringr)

# loading data
data <- fread("data/Tombaugh_Export_LTR.txt")

# transforming data
setnames(data, "Date Digital", "date_digital")
setnames(data, "Date created", "date_created")
setnames(data, "Date modified", "date_modified")
setcolorder(data, c("date_created", "date_modified", "date_digital"))

data[, year_created:=as.numeric(str_extract(date_created, "\\d{4}"))]
data[, year_modified:=as.numeric(str_extract(date_modified, "\\d{4}"))]
data[, year_digital:=as.numeric(str_extract(date_digital, "\\d{4}"))]

annual_counts_created <- na.omit(data[, .(annual_count=.N),
                                      by=year_created][order(year_created)])
annual_counts_modified <- na.omit(data[, .(annual_count=.N),
                                      by=year_modified][order(year_modified)])
annual_counts_digital <- na.omit(data[, .(annual_count=.N),
                                      by=year_digital][order(year_digital)])

annual_counts_created[, type:="Created"]
setnames(annual_counts_created, "year_created", "year")
annual_counts_modified[, type:="Modified"]
setnames(annual_counts_modified, "year_modified", "year")
annual_counts_digital[, type:="Digitized"]
setnames(annual_counts_digital, "year_digital", "year")

annual_counts <- rbind(annual_counts_created,
                       annual_counts_modified,
                       annual_counts_digital)

annual_counts[, type:=factor(type, levels = c("Digitized",
                                               "Created",
                                               "Modified"))]

# plotting
ggplot(data=annual_counts[annual_count>10,], aes(x=year, y=annual_count)) +
   geom_col(fill = "deeppink4") +
   scale_x_continuous(breaks = seq(2015, 2020)) +
   facet_wrap(~type, ncol=1, scales="free_y") +
   labs(x="Year", y="Annual Count of Pages")
```

the column names for the three columns, to "date_digital," "date_created," and "date_modified," and then the function **setcolorder()** to place all three column in the leftmost position in the table, again for easier examining of data. Yet again, create a new column for each type by extracting four-digit year values from dates, with use of the function **str_extract()** and the regular expressions pattern **"\\d{4}"**. In the next step, create three tables with annual counts of time events for each type. Using the function **na.omit()**, remove all rows with missing values.

In order to produce a multifaceted plot with annual counts, take two additional steps. First, in each of three annual count tables, create a new column, "type," storing the type of time event ("Digital," "Created," or "Modified"). You need the column "type" in order to later split the display into term-specific subplots. Next, stack the three annual count tables vertically (to produce the table "annual_counts"), but before doing that, change the names of the columns storing the year value for each type to the common column name "year." To do this, use the function **setnames()**. In the next step, define the ordering in column "type" using the function **factor()** with argument **level** set to a list of types in the preferred chronological order ("Digitized," "Created," "Modified"). The complete data set used for plot 11 is shown in table 3.15.

For plotting, call the function **ggplot()** with the data table "annual_counts" as **data**. In the aesthetics layer, use the function **aes()** to define *x* and *y* axes as "year" and "annual_count" respectively. Next, with the function **geom_col()**, define the geometry of the plot as bar chart, with filling color **"deeppink4"**. Then use the function **scale_x_continuous()** to define the locations of tick marks, by setting the parameter **breaks** to a sequence between 2015 and 2020 (**breaks = seq(2015, 2020)**).

In the next step, call the function **facet_wrap()** to place the three histograms, defined by the values in column "type" (**~ type**) together on one plot. Arrange subplots in one column (**ncol=1**), and allow vertical scales to be optimized independently for each subplot (**scales="free_y"**). Finally, define axis labels using the function **labs()**.

Question 12: What Are Some Problems in the Metadata Fields?

Plot 12 (figure 3.19) is a horizontal bar chart for series counts displaying missing values and issues with series names, such as misplaced or absent commas. The chart demonstrates what the data we work with really look like and thus helps to identify recurrent problems in metadata descriptions. Based on visualizations like the one in figure 3.19, problems with messy metadata are quickly detected and fixed.

After loading packages and data, create a new column, "series_category," by extracting from the column "Series" all characters up to the first occurrence of a comma. For this, call the function **str_remove()** with regular expression pattern **",.*"**.

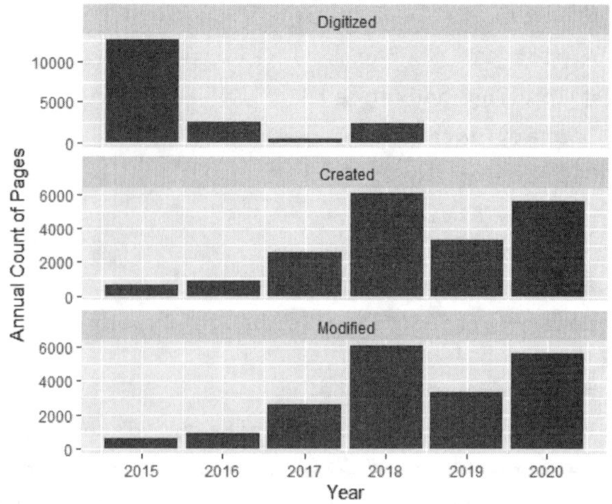

Figure 3.18
Plot 11—set of histograms showing the collection's development

Next, calculate counts of records by unique values in the column "series_category" and store the results in the table "count_serie_category. Table 3.16 shows a fragment of data subjected to plotting.

At this point, feed the rows of "count_series_category" with values smaller than 120 pages (**[count<120,]**) as **data** to the **ggplot()** function. In the aesthetics function (**aes()**), map axis *x* to the column "series_category" (reordered by corresponding counts) and axis *y* to "count." Next, by calling the function **geom_bar()**, define the geometry layer as bar chart, with filling color **"deeppink4"**.

Next, *x* and *y* axes are swapped using the function **coord_flip()**. Set the plot title with the function **ggtitle()**. Finally, with the function **theme()**, define the title's center location (**hjust=0.5**) and font size (**size=12**).

R Shiny—Engaging Library Users in Producing Visualizations without Writing Code

R Shiny opens the analytical and visual power of the R programming language to users who do not have any background in coding. With an interactive user interface (UI), R Shiny allows users to formulate specific questions about digital collections and address those questions with visualizations.

There are two components of an R Shiny application: UI and server. UI, usually a web page, is composed of input and output panels. With input panels, including objects such as sliders, date ranges, drop-down menus,

R SCRIPT FOR PLOT 12

```
# plot_12
# loading packages
library(data.table)
library(ggplot2)
library(stringr)

# loading data
data <- fread("data/Tombaugh_Export_LTR.txt")

# transforming data
data[, series_category:=str_remove(Series, ",.*")]

counts_series_category <- data[, .(count=.N),
                               by=series_category][order(count,
                                                         decreasing = TRUE)]

#plotting
ggplot(counts_series_category[count<120,],
       aes(x=reorder(series_category, count),
           y=count)) +
    geom_col(fill = "deeppink4") +
    coord_flip() +
    labs(y="Total count", x="Series Category") +
    ggtitle("Metadata issues") +
    theme(plot.title=element_text(hjust=0.5, size=12))
```

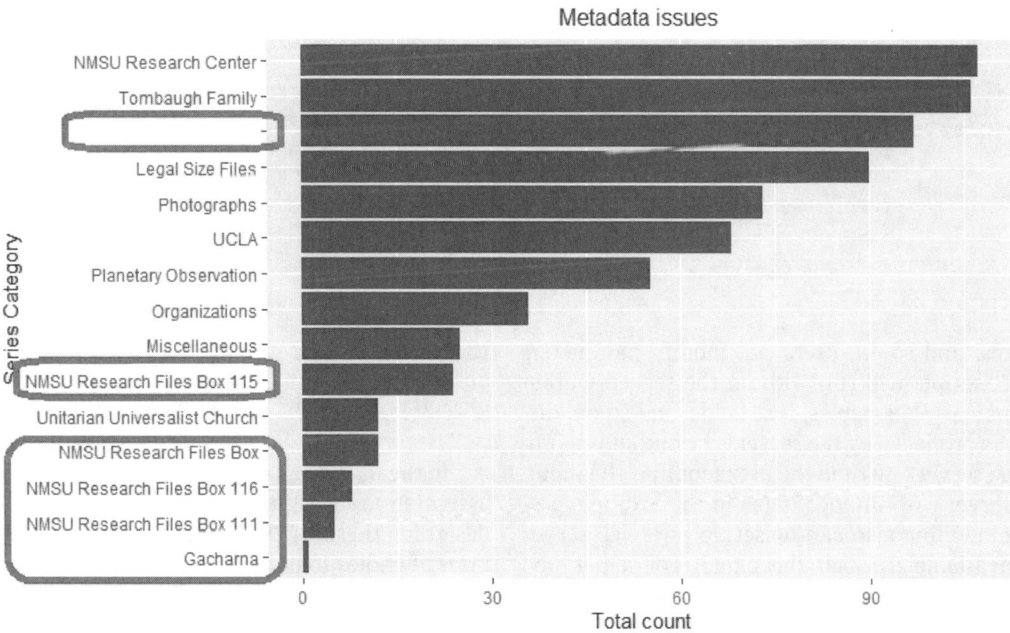

Figure 3.19
Plot 12—horizontal bar chart showing problems with collection's metadata

R SCRIPT FOR PLOTS 13A AND 13B

```
# plot_13
# loading packages
library(shiny)
library(data.table)
library(ggplot2)

# defining user interface
ui <- fluidPage(
    tags$style(type = 'text/css',
               ".selectize-input { font-size: 16px; line-height: 16px;}
               .selectize-dropdown { font-size: 16px; line-height: 16px; }
               label {font-weight: 500; font-size: 24px; }"),

    titlePanel(
      h1("Series Histogram", align = "center")
    ),

    sidebarPanel(
      selectInput(inputId = "series_subset",
                  label = h3("Select series subset"),
                  choices = list("Professional",
                                 "Personal")),

      dateRangeInput(inputId = "dates",
                     label = "Select date range",
                     start = as.Date("1900-01-01"),
                     end = as.Date("2000-12-31"))
    ),

    mainPanel(
      plotOutput(outputId = "series_bar_chart")
    )

)
```

checkboxes, and so on, users can modify parameters that the R scripts will run with on the server. Output panels, such as plots, tables, text fields, and so on, display results produced by the server. The output is modified by the server any time the user modifies the input.

The server can run locally (as in the example presented below), but also can be set up as a web server and be available through the cloud. For a detailed introduction to R Shiny, please check the tutorial on the RStudio platform.[11]

An R Shiny app can start from the following template:[12]

```
ui <- fluidPage()
server <- function(input, output) {}
shinyApp(ui = ui, server = server)
```

In the **`fluidPage()`** function, set the page layout by assigning to its arguments different UI objects. While designing these UI objects, call input and output functions of choice to define the performance of the whole page. All analysis and visualizations take place in the **`server()`** function based on **`input`**. The results are assigned to **`output`**. Finally, in the **`shinyApp()`**, the user interface is connected with the server.

Plots 13a and 13b (figure 3.20 and 3.21) show

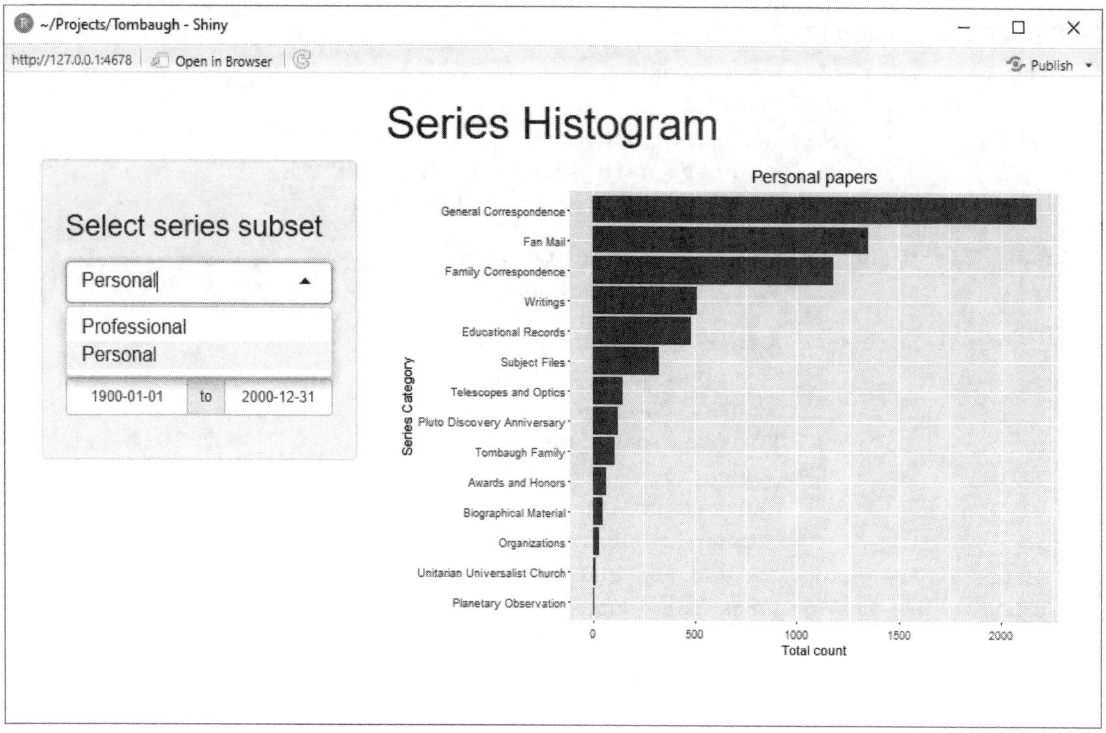

Figure 3.20
Plot 13a—interactive series histogram 1

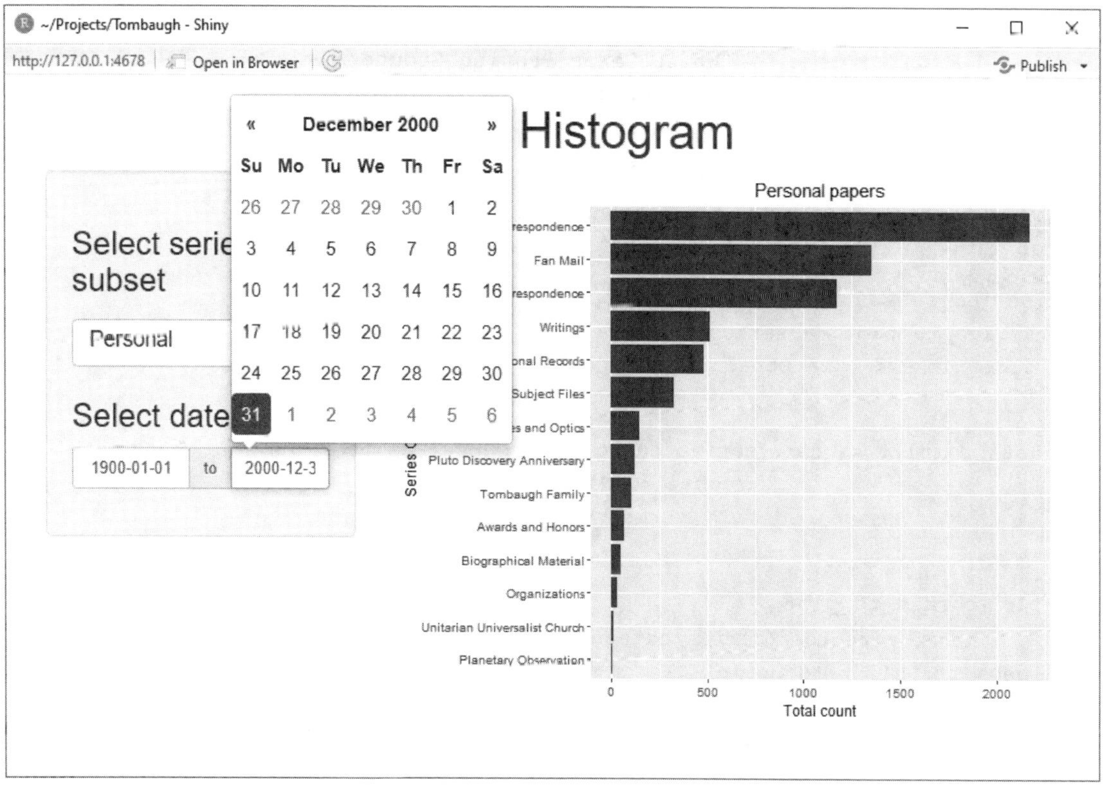

Figure 3.21
Plot 13b—interactive series histogram 2

R SCRIPT FOR PLOTS 13A AND 13B, continued

```
# defining function called by server
series_histogram <- function(data,
                             series_subset = "Professional",
                             start_date = as.Date("1900-01-01"),
                             end_date = as.Date("2000-01-01")) {

    data <- data[year_original >= year(start_date) &
                 year_original <= year(end_date),]

    series_personal <- c("General Correspondence",
                         "Family Correspondence",
                         "Fan Mail",
                         "Biographical Material",
                         "Educational Records",
                         "Subject Files",
                         "Planetary Observation",
                         "Telescopes and Optics",
                         "Organizations",
                         "Pluto Discovery Anniversary",
                         "Awards and Honors",
                         "Tombaugh Family",
                         "Unitarian Universalist Church",
                         "Writings")

    series_professional <- c("Lowell Observatory",
                             "Arizona State Teachers College",
                             "UCLA",
                             "White Sands Proving Ground",
                             "New Mexico State University",
                             "NMSU Physical Science Lab",
                             "NMSU Research Files")

    series_to_plot <- series_professional
    plot_title <- "Professional papers"

    if(series_subset == "Personal") {
      series_to_plot <- series_personal
      plot_title <- "Personal papers"
    }

    counts_to_plot <- data[series_category %in% series_to_plot,
                           .(count = .N),
                           by = series_category][order(count,
                                                       decreasing = TRUE)]

    ggplot(counts_to_plot,
           aes(x = reorder(series_category, count), y = count)) +
      geom_col(fill = "deeppink4") +
      coord_flip() +
      labs(y = "Total count", x = "Series Category") +
      ggtitle(plot_title) +
      theme(plot.title = element_text(hjust = 0.5, size = 14))

}
```

interactive R Shiny versions of plots 4a and 4b that compare volumes of documents in selected series in personal and professional papers.

As before, first load packages and define the user interface. The arguments to the **fluidPage()** function, which sets the page layout, are **tags$style()**, **titlePanel()**, **sidebarPanel()**, **and mainPanel()**. Using **tags$style()**, define font sizes used in select list **(selectInput())** and date range **(dateRangeInput())** input controls. In **titlePanel()**, set the title of the page and its center location. In **sidebarPanel()**, define two input panels—for the select list (**selectInput()**) and the date range (**dateRangeInput()**). In both, set unique names for these inputs (**inputId**) by which they are identified in other parts of the app code, as well as their labels (**label**), which are displayed in the UI. These labels should help explain the functions of these panels. There are also input-specific arguments. For **selectInput()**, it is **choices**, defining a list of available values to select from. For **dateRangeInput()** these are **start** and **end** dates, by default set to "1900-01-01" and "2000-12-31" respectively.

In **main_panel()**, by calling the function **plotOutput()**, you define the type of output as a plot. You also define the plot's **outputId** (as "series_bar_chart") by which it can be identified in other parts of the app code.

The function **series_histogram()**, called by the server, replicates the R script for plots 4a and 4b (see the R script for Plots 13a and 13b, continued). Here it produces the chart depending on three parameters, **series_subset** (either "Professional" or "Personal," the former being the default) as well as **start_date** and **end_date** with default values "1900-01-01" and "2000-01-01" respectively. After defining the lists "series_personal" and "series_professional," set **series_to_plot** by default to "series_professional" (and, similarly, the plot title to "Professional papers"). If the argument **series_subset** is instead "Personal," set **series_to_plot** to "series_personal" and the plot title to "Personal papers." Next, produce the data table "counts_to_plot" with document counts for unique values in column "series_category" for the selected subset of series. Finally, plot the counts in a horizontal bar chart using the function **ggplot()**.

```
# defining server
server <- function(input, output) {
     output$series_bar_chart
     <- renderPlot({
       series_histogram(data=fread("data/
       data_4_shiny_s.csv"),
          series_subset =
          input$series_subset,
          start_date =
             as.Date(input$dates[1]),
             end_date =
             as.Date(input$dates[2]))
     })
}
# launching application, connecting user
interface with server
shinyApp(ui = ui, server = server)
```

In the second major component, the definition of function **server()**, you assign the plot produced by the function **series_histogram()** to output "series_bar_chart."

Besides the argument **data**, assigned directly as the output of the function **fread()**, the remaining arguments are assigned from input, using the relevant input identifiers.

Finally, launch the R Shiny app by putting together the UI and server code with the function **shinyApp()**.

Notes

1. Kevin Schindler and Will Grundy, *Pluto and Lowell Observatory: A History of Discovery at Flagstaff* (Charleston, SC: History Press, 2018); "Kevin Schindler," Lowell Observatory, accessed July 10, 2020, https://lowell.edu/author/kevin-schindler/.
2. "Jackson-Gwilt Medal," Royal Astronomical Society, accessed July 10, 2020, https://ras.ac.uk/awards-and-grants/awards/jackson-gwilt-medal.
3. "I Heart Pluto Festival," Lowell Observatory, accessed July 10, 2020, https://lowell.edu/i-heart-pluto-festival.
4. "Clyde W. Tombaugh Collection," NMSU Library, accessed July 12, 2020, https://lib.nmsu.edu/exhibits/tombaugh/bio.shtml.
5. New Mexico Museum of Space History home page, accessed July 12, 2020, https://www.nmspacemuseum.org/.
6. "Tombaugh Postdoctoral Fellowship," NMSU Astronomy, accessed July 15, 2020, http://astronomy.nmsu.edu/fellowships-awards/tombaugh-fellowship/.
7. "Clyde W. Tombaugh," New Mexico Museum of Space History, accessed July 16, 2020, https://www.nmspacemuseum.org/inductee/clyde-w-tombaugh/.
8. "Register of the Clyde W. Tombaugh Papers, 1908–2000," Rocky Mountain Online Archive, accessed July 16, 2020, https://rmoa.unm.edu/docviewer.php?docId=nmlcu1ms0407.xml#hit.
9. Wikipedia, s.v. "Regular expression," last modified July, 29, 2020, 06:09 (UTC), https://en.wikipedia.org/wiki/Regular_expression.
10. Google Maps Platform, accessed August 8, 2020, https://cloud.google.com/maps-platform/.
11. "Learn Shiny," Shiny from RStudio, https://shiny.rstudio.com/tutorial/.
12. "Learn Shiny."

## Chapter 4

Conclusion and Resources

In the context of the data-driven knowledge economy and ubiquitous screen culture, the role of visualization as a communication tool has increased considerably. Visuals clearly and effectively convey factual information extracted from data. But the power of the visuals does not stop there. Visual representations of data also reveal patterns and trends hidden in data and thus enable further exploration and addressing new research questions.

One way of looking at library digital collections is to view them as repositories of digital data that can be explored and analyzed. Visualization as a method for exploring digital content provides unique insights into collections for both library patrons and collection curators. Applying visualization allows viewing a digital collection through analysis of its data. As more and more technologies have become available to facilitate the creation of visualizations, this method for exploring data and communicating their findings is now at our fingertips.

The R programming language has been specifically designed to support analysis and visualization of data. R is free, open source, and actively supported by an established community of developers, coders, and enthusiasts. R also is relatively easy to learn and experiment with.

As demonstrated in this report, a few lines of R code may instantly create charts that address a range of questions regarding a digital collection, starting from content overviews and ending at identifying specific metadata issues. Eighteen visualizations of the Clyde W. Tombaugh Papers digital collection described in this report directly reflect and help interpret the content of this collection and also indirectly shed some light on the life and career of a scientist. Based on these visualizations, new findings emerged.

As discussed throughout this report, visualizations provide holistic views of collection content and invite users to engage with historic documents actively and creatively. At the very least, visualizations fill the gap between an item-level description found on a digital collection's display and an extensive collection-level description issued in an archival finding aid. But visualization may also inform the creation of metadata. Now when we know what information is needed to produce useful charts, we may reevaluate metadata elements that describe our collections.

This report is meant to encourage the creation of visualizations for digital collections and inspire further exploration of collection data. R scripts, provided along with explanations of code, are to serve only as examples of possible solutions.

Resources

Installing R and RStudio

- The R Project for Statistical Computing website, https://www.r-project.org/
- CRAN Mirrors, https://cran.r-project.org/mirrors.html
- RStudio website, https://rstudio.com/
- How to Articles, RStudio Support, https://support.rstudio.com/hc/en-us/categories/200035113-Documentation

Learning R

- What is R? Introduction to R on r-project.org, https://www.r-project.org/about.html
- R Manuals on r-project.org, https://cran.r-project.org/manuals.html
- Documentation on r-project.org, https://www.r-project.org/other-docs.html
- *The R Journal* home page, https://journal.r-project.org/
- *The R Blog*, https://developer.r-project.org/Blog/public/
- The R Foundation @ Twitter, https://twitter.com/_R_Foundation
- Books Related to R on r-project.org, https://www.r-project.org/doc/bib/R-books.html

Other Books

- Hadley Wickham and Garrett Grolemund, *R for Data Science: Import, Tidy, Transform, Visualize and Model Data* (Sebastopol, CA: O'Reilly Media, 2017).
- J. D. Long, and Paul Teetor, *R Cookbook: Proven Recipes for Data Analysis, Statistics and Graphics* (Sebastopol, CA: O'Reilly Media, 2019).

Platforms That Provide Courses on R

- Codecademy, https://www.codecademy.com/
- Coursera, https://www.coursera.org/
- DataCamp, https://www.datacamp.com/
- Quick-R by DataCamp, https://www.statmethods.net/
- edX, https://www.edx.org/
- Udacity, https://www.udacity.com/
- Udemy, https://www.udemy.com/
- Library Carpentry, https://librarycarpentry.org/

Learning RStudio

- How to Articles, RStudio Support, https://support.rstudio.com/hc/en-us/categories/200035113-Documentation
- RStudio Cheatsheets, https://rstudio.com/resources/cheatsheets/
- RStudio Essentials, https://rstudio.com/collections/rstudio-essentials/
- RStudio Webinars, https://rstudio.com/resources/webinars/
- *RStudio Blog*, https://blog.rstudio.com/
- RStudio Community, https://community.rstudio.com/

Cleaning Data

- OpenRefine, https://openrefine.org/
- Library Carpentry, https://librarycarpentry.org/

Selecting Charts

- The Extreme Presentation Method, by Andrew Abela, https://extremepresentation.com/
- The Data Visualisation Catalogue, by Severino Ribecca, https://datavizcatalogue.com/index.html
- The Visualization Universe, by Anna Vital, Mark Vital, Alexander Vushkan, Simon Roger, and Alberto Cairo, http://visualizationuniverse.com/
- Chartopedia, by AnyChart, https://www.anychart.com/chartopedia
- From Data to Viz, by Yan Holtz and Conor Healy, https://www.data-to-viz.com/
- Scott Berinato, *Good Charts: The HRB Guide to Making Smarter, More Persuasive Data Visualizations*, (Boston: Harvard Business Review Press, 2016).

Library Technology REPORTS

Upcoming Issues	
February/ March 57:2	**Mobile Technology in Libraries** by David Lee King
April 57:3	**Video Accessibility** by Carli Spina
May/June 57:4	**Creating Adaptable Digital Preservation Workflows** by Erin Baucom